IN SPITE
OF THE
ODDS

A True Inspirational Journey from
Walk-on to Full Scholarship at Ole Miss

RICHIE CONTARTESI

Defy the Odds Publishing
1562 First Ave #205-2981
New York, NY 10028-4004

Ordering Information:
Quantity sales. Special discounts are available on quantity purchases by corporations, associations, and others. For details, contact the publisher at the address above.
Orders by U.S. trade bookstores and wholesalers. Please contact Defy the Odds Publishing: Order@DefytheOddsPublishing.com.

Printed in the United States of America

In Spite Of The Odds: A True Inspirational Journey from Walk-on to Full Scholarship at Ole Miss / Richie Contartesi
www.EarnAScholarship.com
ISBN: 978-0-9966185-1-9

Contents

CHAPTER 1

Building a Foundation

MY STORY BEGINS with an average kid growing up in the suburbs of West Palm Beach, Florida. The neighborhood was perfect because there were kids everywhere, tons of kids. It just so happened, though, that out of our big circle of friends, I was one of the youngest and the smallest. Watching some of those home videos are still hilarious to this day.

I started showing some athletic ability at a really young age. I was able to ride a two-wheel bike at three years old. While I was growing up, my best friend, Zach Legato, lived right across the street from me. He was a year older, bigger, faster, and stronger than me—and very athletic. Having him as a friend was great for me because, as I now look back and see, he was one of the real reasons I was able to achieve one of my ultimate goals. He may not have known it, but he was always pushing me in sports, and I was always trying to keep up with him. We would play one-on-one sports all the time, and because he was bigger, faster, and stronger, it was a challenge for me to find ways to win—but I would. That kept things interesting, and more importantly, it kept the games flowing.

The other neighborhood guys we hung out with were older than both Zach and me—much older. One of my neighbors, Thomas Raab, lived right next door and played football for the high school team. I remember that one day, running around in the front yard wearing his helmet, I ran into a tree chasing a football; his helmet was so big it flopped around and landed sideways. I was eight years old at the time.

Growing up, we would play in the street or the front yard for hours and hours, just throwing the football, catching the football, throwing the football, catching the football; and I really attribute my hand-eye coordination to that—learning to catch everything that was thrown my way. After years of "practice," or what I considered playing, it was just natural. I didn't drop the ball once in a high school game, and I believe that all that practice, along with my love of the game, contributed to my success.

Zach and I invented our own games. On Sundays, we would wear New York Jets football jerseys and imitate our favorite players. He was wide receiver Keyshawn Johnson and I was wide receiver Wayne Chrebet. These were our favorite players, and the players who matched our athletic abilities. Keshawn was taller, faster, and stronger than Chrebet, but Chrebet had better hands and was "the playmaker" (more about being a playmaker later). We'd find the biggest bushes we could throughout the neighborhood, and one of us would run and the other one would throw the ball upward; we would jump and catch the ball, fly into the bush and bounce out—sometimes the bush would make us flip.

At the time, it was all about having fun. I would call him at seven o'clock in the morning to ask if he wanted to play "bushes," and then we would play for hours. When I look back today, I see that we were unknowingly doing an awesome "drill" that led to the ability to go over the middle easily, without fear. The average person—kid or parent—would have thought we were crazy. After doing this "drill" of ours, I would come home with scars, scratches, and scrapes. Even during commercials and halftime of the Jets games we watched, we would run outside and play "bushes." We never played inside when I was a kid—unless we were grounded or it was pouring rain, and even then we often found ways to play outside. We would skimboard on the golf course behind our neighborhood or play tackle football through the puddles. We didn't care. I thought not being allowed to play outside was the worst possible punishment. I was having the time of my life. And then fifth grade happened.

Fifth grade was a very difficult year. I had trouble concentrating in class and when doing my homework. I think the problem worsened when my parents separated and eventually divorced. The combination of divorce and poor grades eventually led to an implosion of sorts for me when I failed the grade. Yep, I failed fifth grade. I was embarrassed, demoralized. My parents and I spent the summer developing a strategy for me to get back on track.

I was fortunate to attend a small specialized school with only two other students in my grade. The school curriculum was very focused, and the teachers helped me improve my learning and studying habits. In one year, I compensated for my fifth-grade deficiencies and completed all the required course work to pass sixth grade. I worked hard, learned how to concentrate, and learned some valuable life lessons; and then I was ready to tackle seventh grade.

I started the year playing both baseball and football. I had a passion for football, but inside I knew baseball was becoming less important. As in the past, my dad signed me up for baseball but the excitement was gone. When I was very young, about four years old, baseball was fun, but as I got older, well, I was just bored. I didn't enjoy the game anymore, and I certainly didn't love it. I wanted to play football. I even tried to quit in the middle of the season, but my dad wouldn't let me. I remember sitting in the car on the way home from a practice, telling my dad, "The only reason I am playing baseball is for you." Now, I don't think I meant this, but I was really unhappy. My dad said, "You're not quitting, and you are going to finish the season. Once the season is over, you can move on." This taught me a lesson that would come into play often on the journey to my dreams, and would even save me a few times along the way: never quit and never give up, no matter how difficult the climb. There was another important lesson I learned during little league baseball, and it came from one of my best coaches, Mike Jalad. He always asked, "What's the most important play?" We would answer, "The next play!" This has stuck with me throughout my whole career in sports and, currently, in business.

I don't know why, but throughout my little league football career, every team I was on was horrible. It seemed I was one of the best players on each team, and not because I was the fastest or the biggest—I was always below average in size. But one thing I learned in little league was to love hitting, and I worked harder and hit harder than most of the player on the team, no matter how big they were. My first coach said I was "the steal of the draft." Because my athleticism at the tryout hadn't been eye popping, I'd been drafted low, but when we put the pads on, I rocked everyone. I remember the first time I ever put the pads on and had hitting practice. I was running people over and hitting people left and right. My dad woke me up the next day for church and I was so sore I literally could not get out of bed. I think I rolled out of bed, but I ended up missing church. I loved playing defense, loved playing offense, loved special teams, and was always trying to run over people. I just loved hitting. And that love was what helped me excel when most everyone else was scared. I found ways to score and win games where we could, but the fact remained that I wasn't on the best of teams.

My third year, I played with a running back by the name of Brandon Pendergrass. He was an amazing athlete and his dad was our coach. Lonnie Pendergrass had played in the NFL. The two of them taught me a lot about the game and, specifically, the position of running back. Brandon went on to break high school records and had a tremendous career at Wake Forest and then with the Baltimore Ravens. Playing against him in high school was a mission, but I am glad I learned what I did from him and his dad.

Right before I entered high school, I dislocated and fractured my elbow. It was completely disconnected and required surgery. To this day, there are some weightlifting and athletic moves I can't do because of it, and it's still tender and aches from time to time. This injury made playing in high school a little rough, especially in my freshman year. In high school, you have the freshman, junior varsity, and varsity teams, and through camp, I ended up working my way to the freshman-team position of starting quarterback. I had played a similar position through little league, because they usually selected the more athletic players for quarterback. Now, I was never trained to be a drop-back passer and or to learn the quarterback position correctly, but I played as an athlete running the option. At my high school, this usually doesn't happen. Usually by your freshman year, they are looking to mold a drop-back quarterback, and the athletes move to receiver and running back.

I had wanted to play quarterback, and I earned the starting role my freshman year at Wellington High School in Wellington, Florida. We weren't very good—I think we won one or two games—but toward the end of the year, I ended up playing safety as well. Happily, I was able to keep the hitting going. At this time I was about five feet seven, 140 pounds. My freshman year was really difficult for me as a quarterback, because the linemen were a lot bigger and I couldn't see over them. The quarterback coach taught me how to look through windows as a smaller quarterback, how to drop back at an angle, and a few other techniques. I used this solution and also examined as much film on Doug Flutie as possible. You would be surprised at what you can learn from studying film, even just on regular TV. Part of freshman year was a good experience, but overall our win/loss ratio wasn't good.

Toward the end of my freshman year, I found out I'd be attending Palm Beach Central High School, a new school in Wellington. The new school was very different from Wellington High School because of the demographic and socioeconomic diversity of the student population. It was a melting pot. In my first year, through hard work and persistence, I found myself as the starting varsity quarterback in a Division 6 high school. That was a big deal. Division 6 featured the largest high schools in the county, each school stacked with the best players, including a number of D1 prospects. I was, again, probably one of the smallest kids on the team, but Head Coach John Timmins believed in me. He was extremely hard on me—harder than he was on any of the other players. At the end of the season, not only did I earn a special award but he also paid me with the highest compliment at the awards banquet. I will never forget his words, mentoring, and how he held me accountable for my play and actions. It was all worth it.

Unfortunately, we didn't win a single game—we went 0 and 10 my sophomore year—but I always found ways to keep the team together, and I played decently well for a fifteen-year-old playing with seventeen- and eighteen-year-olds. Though I started out as quarterback, I would also move to receiver from time to time. Crazily enough, I led the team in passing yards and receiving yards. Losing all ten games was tough, but being a leader and working through adversity was something I faced in the past in my football career. This was probably my biggest character-building and humbling year, at least until I stepped foot on the campus of Ole Miss. I am telling you, it was tough going to keep practicing while constantly losing games—and not just losing, but getting crushed. One away game, against Centennial High School, we lost 77-6. Since I was the starting quarterback, I was the one who took the blame, not to mention the wrath, from Head Coach Timmins. He would rip me a new ear nearly every practice. It was a trying year, but I learned a lot about resilience and dealing with rough times.

The other reason I did well: my neighbor, Zach Legato, whom I'd grown up with. Remember "bushes"? He was my number-one receiver. Being a year older, he had always played in the older league, but now the only thing left was varsity, so we were finally playing together. All those years of throwing the ball back and forth to each other and being teammates in all our street leagues paid off. When he ran around, I knew not only exactly where he was but also the when, how, and why of his movements, and I was able to drill him. As you can imagine, that was a sweet situation.

I will never forget the awards ceremony after my sophomore season. We'd had the most painful year, not winning a single game. I had given my all to the team, but since we were a new school, we didn't have any seniors, and man, had this been a challenge. I was the leader and a focal point of the team. I'd taken a lot of punishment in practice and during games had been benched for numerous reasons. Then at the ceremony, once all of the awards were given out, there was only one left: offensive player of the year. I knew it was coming because the award before was defensive player of the year. Even though I had led the team in passing and receiving, I knew there was no way that I would receive this award as a sophomore, not with the superior size and talent ahead of me. I thought J'Mayne Christian, our running back and the best athlete on the team hands down, would win the award. My head coach, John Timmins, said something that put my work ethic and attitude in perspective. He started out his speech by saying, "If I could put this player's work ethic in a bottle and sell it, it would be priceless. No matter what ups and downs he suffered, he came to practice ready to play, and he never quit when most players would." He continued to speak, but this resonated with me the most. When, at the end, he called my name, goose bumps started at my toes and traveled to the tip of my head. He handed me my first big award in football; before this, there had been the small trophies you get for little league every year. His statement still replays in my mind every day. It defined the person I was in college, and today it defines me in business.

Going into the off-season of my junior year, a new quarterback transferred in from another school—and he was really good. He was a well-established "actual quarterback." What do I mean by this? Unlike me, he had been training as a drop back and roll out passer. My coach didn't want to take the obvious route and play him though, both because he didn't want me off the field and because the new guy had transferred based on "off-the-field" issues at his previous school. Regardless, the goal was to win games, so

Coach Timmins ended up telling me I needed to learn receiver. I said to myself, "Okay, I could play slot receiver." I could even see this as a long-term arrangement, regarding college and the NFL. It had never crossed my mind that I couldn't play quarterback in college, but when I thought about playing receiver, it made much more sense. That whole summer I worked with the new quarterback and focused on learning receiver and learning timing with him.

While I was going into my junior year, Zach was going into his senior, and we were now the two core starting receivers. After all those years playing together, we were now starting and varsity receivers at the same time. Coincidence? I don't think so. I still believe it was the countless hours that we considered just fun that accounted for our developing the special skills we both needed to arrive where we eventually did. At the end of the day, he was bigger and faster than me, but for some reason, I always had a knack for making big plays. Whenever it was time to make a big play, you could assume the ball was coming my way. This was the biggest difference between us, in my opinion. I had this intangible skill to make the big play.

That brings us to my junior year, Palm Beach Central High School's second year. We again had a rough start to the season, but something changed with the team. In week six, there was a different aura in the air. The team felt different; there was just more energy.

It was homecoming week and we were playing Santaluces High School, which at the time was tied for first place in the district. The game was very low scoring, and at half time, we were up 6-0. We still had not won a game in the school's existence up to this point, in year two. We couldn't move the ball at all on offense, but our defense kept us in the game.

At half time, before we went back on the field, I gave a quick speech telling the team that this was it—we were going to pull this off in front of a large homecoming crowd. When the team ran out of the tunnel, there was a sense of confidence and camaraderie. When we got back on the field we stayed positive despite continuing to struggle with offense. Our defense held them to 0 all game until the last three minutes, when one of their stars broke loose for a touchdown. This was tough, but we had time. That sensibility of my intangible skill started to trickle down my arms. Yup: it was time to make a big play. It was 3rd and 16 with less than two minutes left in the game, and we were on our own 40-yard line. Head Coach John Timmins called a play that was actually meant for the tight end running a corner route; Zach and I were on the back side. I had a post route, Zach a 10 yard in route. Our quarterback snapped the ball and rolled to his left looking for the tight end, the safety came down on the tight end, and I ran right past my corner and safety. My quarterback saw me and let it rip. It was a 45-yard pass in the air. I reached. I caught it. I didn't hear a sound or feel a thing. I was so in the zone that I couldn't think, speak, or hear. It is the wildest feeling in the world.

Immediately after I stood up from being tackled, it all hit me. The noise of the crowd screaming, the chanting, my teammates jumping on top of me. We ended up holding them for the final minute of the game, and we won the school's first game—against the number-one team in the district on homecoming at that. It was worth all those losses. The stands cleared as everyone ran onto the field and celebrated; it was exactly what you see on TV after a huge upset. I remember running up to my dad as soon as the game ended and just breaking down. I had waited more than a year and a half for this day, and I made the catch that won the game.

Bragging about the high school glory days? I suppose, but I can proudly say I led Palm Beach Central High School to its first win in the school's history. To this day, having watched the film over and over, I'm not sure how it happened, but I am 99.9 percent sure that I wasn't faster than these guys. It's crazy when you see it on the film. The quarterback threw it upward and I just jumped into another gear and made the catch. The rush of the fans was incredible and unforgettable. Working hard to earn anything was becoming the norm in my life.

We ended up winning the next three games. I'd known that once we won our first, other victories would just start pouring in. Practice was fun, school was fun, and we had a real sense of love for each other. We didn't have a chance at the playoffs, unfortunately, but we ended the season—and entered the start of the new off-season—on a high note. I didn't win any awards that year, but Zach was named offensive player of the year as a senior. I was happy for him and also determined to win the award the following year.

The next year—my final year at the school and my third as

a captain—we lost a lot of our key players from the year before. I even played both ways. I started at receiver, defensive back, punt returner, and kick returner. My goal was to bring this team together and finally break into the playoffs. I remember that when I got to camp, I was in tip-top shape, but some of my fellow teammates were not. I was extremely mad and held everyone accountable by having the team run extra drills. As a captain, and simply as a player on the team, I took charge and ran extra along with them to show how much I cared.

We didn't do too badly as the year began; we started off slow, but things had begun to pick up by week four when, bam, I sprained my ankle. It was homecoming, with our new "black" jerseys on, and I was so excited for the game. The color of our regular uniforms were red and pewter. The black jerseys were a surprise from the football boosters. It was a muggy and rainy night. On the first play the quarterback threw me the ball, I caught it, and then I felt a helmet crash right into my ankle. I felt my ankle bend and I heard a pop and I knew I was done. I couldn't even hop off the field. When I tried tapping on my ankle, I knew for certain there was no way I could walk on it. Unfortunately, I needed a cast and ended up missing the next five games. I may have gained some really good stats in the first few weeks, but breaking my ankle midway through the season was a killer. However, because of a hurricane at the end of the year—of all the things to bring me luck—our final game was pushed back two weeks, and I was able to play.

We needed to win this game to get into the playoffs, and it was time. When I'd broken my ankle, all of the letters I was receiving from D1 colleges immediately stopped. I didn't think or care about it. I just continued to rehab my ankle and get ready for the final game. I had more than four catches, including a huge 4th and 20 that we converted to take the lead at the end of the 4th quarter. Seem familiar? Well, it was and it wasn't. The opposing team drove down the field and, with time expiring, kicked a 40-yard field goal and won the game.

It was over. High school football was over. My goal to lead the team to the playoffs failed. We lost, I lost. Now not only was it over, but every school that had been interested in me, every bigger Division I school, dropped me from their list. It hit me once the season was over and I had time to think. I was worried, sad, and confused. More importantly, I was disappointed and down on myself.

One rule Coach John Timmins had for our team always stuck with me; and while it may sound very simple, it took me a long way toward doing things right. He said, "Be where you're supposed to be when you are supposed to be there, and do what you are supposed to be doing." Basically, if you are going to practice, be there early. When you are at practice, practice hard. There's no reason to play around at practice when you have the rest of the day to do whatever you want. Whether you are at school, at practice, watching film, or in the weight room, make sure that you are 100 percent engaged and that you are always bettering yourself. Don't goof around with your teammates and waste time. You are there to get better, reach your dreams, and help the team win. Give the team your all, and your team will give back to you. Lead by example. Show that you are committed and you care. If you do this, life will have no other choice but to reward you.

When the season ended and high school football was over, Coach Timmins took me aside and said he was going to miss me, and that he was going to do everything in his power to get me a shot in college.

At the end of the season, we had the standard ceremony. I was so worried about getting into college and continuing my football career, though, that the award ceremony was the last thing on my mind. I just needed a chance to play D1 football. As the ceremony went on, I started paying more attention to the moment and enjoying being in the same room with my teammates one last time. After the initial awards, the coach, as always, went into the awards for defensive player of the year—which went to my best friend, Alex Roth—and then offensive player of the year, which went to the other captain, Tyler McDermott. He was a four-year starter at center and an awesome player who ended up playing at Colorado State.

At that point, I thought the ceremony was over and I was just out of luck, but Coach Timmins pulled out one last award. It was an award they'd never given before. He then began describing what this individual did for the team, as a leader and a player on the field. Noticing how the team suffered when this player was not on the field. How the player, even when he couldn't play, did everything possible to help the team from the sidelines. He then proceeded to say that the new award, for most valuable player, went to Richie Contartesi.

I went from low to high pretty quickly. I mean a team MVP

award at a 6A school in Palm Beach County should almost definitely get a D1 scholarship, right? Well, not in my case, unfortunately. Don't get me wrong. I was honored, but I still didn't reach my goal of signing a D1 scholarship.

I had an up-and-down career in high school. My stats were very strong and always flip-flopped with those of other top players in the county, such as Preston Parker and Brandon Heath, both of whom went on to earn D1 scholarships. They were also six feet one and six feet four, respectively. Spraining my ankle and being out for half the season my senior year had been a killer. Calls from colleges stopped, and so did my film and stats.

I was looking for schools in Coach Timmins's office every day after school. I was also talking to him about different schools, filling out forms and applications, and trying anything and everything to get in somewhere. Coach Timmins even made a call to Florida International University (FIU), a small D1 school in Miami. I was in his office when Timmins said he had a player sitting in front of him who "could walk on and who would eventually be a key contributor for you." Timmins then handed me the phone, and the coach proceeded to ask me questions; I don't think I could have sold myself any better. He then told me to come to his office the next day. I was thrilled and so thankful.

I didn't sleep well that night, and the next day, I bolted to Miami only to find that the coach didn't want me on the team after seeing my five-feet-seven, 150-pound frame. I'd no sooner walked in than he said, "Oh sorry. I just filled my last walk on spot." That was it—nothing I could say. He went back into his office and shut the door. Wow, was that a let-down.

As mad as I was after that meeting, I was also determined—to show this coach that he'd just made the biggest mistake of his life. I was extremely motivated. I shot back up to Palm Beach and sat down with Timmins again. We went over a few opportunities with some really small schools. My best friend, Alex Roth, who was the other captain and middle linebacker, and I were both being recruited hard by the best D3 school in the country, Mount Union. So I said, "Heck with it, let's both take a road trip and check it out." At the time, Pierre Garcon, who would become the leading receiver for the Colts and Redskins, was their top player. They tried hard to recruit us when we stayed with them, but at the end of the day, it was D3 and it was far from home.

I also visited Jacksonville University, a D1AA school, on an official visit, meaning they pay for your trip. I wasn't impressed with the campus, the facilities, or the program, but between my size and injury, this was the biggest and best opportunity I had. I even had a few full scholarship offers from D2 schools, but again, I was set on going to the biggest. I ended up signing with Jacksonville University on a partial scholarship. Not only was this not a true D1 school but it was only a partial scholarship. This is where my sideways route to earning a full D1 scholarship began.

CHAPTER 2

Welcome to College Football

I MADE THE DECISION to go to Jacksonville University (JU), and Coach Timmons set up a signing day at my high school. The local newspaper reported the signing, but I didn't feel that it was a big accomplishment, so I didn't make a big deal of it; I just began my preparation. At this point, I was going to use my disappointment to make sure I didn't redshirt. I was determined to play right away, as a true freshman.

Over the summer following my senior year of high school, I trained for about eight weeks at Athlete's Advantage in Wellington, which a friend told me was the best place for conditioning. When I arrived in Jacksonville, I was in really good shape. Well, at least that's how I felt when I first got there. Anyway, Athlete's Advantage was my first exposure to real college conditioning and training.

I was in a workout group with eight Division 1 signees. One recruit, an excellent southern Florida talent, had been offered scholarships from Florida State, the University of Miami, and the University of Florida, but he didn't have the grades. These types of players usually have to go to junior college (JuCo) for the first two years, get their grades together, and then sign with the D1 program that offers them an opportunity.

Athlete's Advantage provided me with an opportunity to train with the best athletes and begin preparing for football at the college level. Not only did I get to play with the best athletes in high school, but I also had the opportunity to train and refine my skills at Athlete's Advantage.

When I first walked into the facility, I was actually a little worried that they were not going to accept me. As it turned out, the coach, who knew all the best players in the area, also knew me, both from newspaper articles and word of mouth.

In my initial work out, I learned that a 110 was a 110-yard "stride," but with my short legs, it was more of a stride-sprint. Standard time for skill positions was fifteen seconds to run the 110 yards with a forty-five second rest. The conditioning we'd done in high school had never been timed and, in my opinion, had always been simple, but in college we had to be prepared to run these 110s.

My second day in the program, the coach informed us we would prepare for our goal of sixteen 110s by starting with ten of them. Each person was teamed with a partner. The partners ran side by side and our times were recorded. My partner was a receiver who signed with North Carolina State (NCSU).

Lucky me, he was six feet four and had the stride of a cheetah. It was okay though; I think the nervousness had my adrenaline running, which in the beginning definitely helped me out. The first three 110s were easy, but after the fourth and fifth repetitions, the entire group was falling out. People were either throwing up or were unable to move. I was in the unable-to-move category. After the fifth rep, my legs hurt so badly I had to lie down. Not one person passed the fifth rep. This was a real eye opener for me—I knew I had a lot of work to do.

Throughout the next seven weeks, we did our normal training for speed, strength, agility, and size, and we proceeded with conditioning toward the end of each session. We added one additional 110 every week. By the end of the eight weeks, I was recognized as one of the hardest workers and earned a lot of respect from the coaches and players. I not only kept up with some of these top athletes but also beat them in some of our timed and weight-lifting drills.

During our final conditioning test, I ran sixteen 110s like it was nothing and walked right out of the facility, not even sore. I was extremely thankful to the coach for the opportunity to be a part of an elite group. Without this intense training, I would have had a really rough start at Jacksonville University.

I wasn't the happiest camper when I did go to Jacksonville University—it had just seemed my only option. I vividly remember driving four hours to the college and not even feeling excited. I felt I had let myself down, that I wasn't reaching my maximum potential. I had always wanted to be the best, and I wasn't happy.

Now, scholarships at JU worked very differently than at most big Division 1 colleges. I wasn't on a full scholarship; mine covered roughly half. As a private school, Jacksonville University was really expensive—even with the scholarship. The dorms were old and needed a lot of work. The rooms smelled of moth balls, the floors were yellow, and in some spots the paint was peeling off the walls. But even though the dorms were a disaster, I ended up meeting one of the most important friends and influences in my life, Dean McNash.

Dean lived in the next room over from me, and immediately we hit it off, discovering we had a ton in common. To this day he is my best friend, and I don't know what I would do without him. He also played at Jacksonville during my first year but during camp incurred an injury that required surgery and ended his promising football career.

Dean had been an all-star high school linebacker for St. Thomas Aquinas, an extremely prestigious team in Ft. Lauderdale, Florida. The best of the best get scholarships there—and he was one of them. After his big injury on his first day in pads at camp, he experienced multiple shoulder problems and underwent numerous surgeries, which in turn stopped him from continuing his football career. One of the biggest things Dean taught me was dieting, which really helped me through my college career. I'll talk more about that later.

On the first day at Jacksonville University, we had a team meeting. The staff did a walkthrough of the antiquated facilities, showing us the locker rooms, training facilities, and other areas. The stadium was old, small, and not as modern as my high school stadium. The coaches said, "Tomorrow is the one-ten test, so go to bed early." We all ate as a team that night, and I went to bed early.

I can't speak for everyone else, but this was my chance to immediately make an impact and show how hard I had worked over the summer. During the test, I ran ten 110s under fourteen seconds and was in the top three every rep. The upperclassmen had to run sixteen 110s. I quickly evaluated who the hard workers were in the receiver group. The next day we officially started camp.

Since it wasn't such a high-end college for football, JU didn't have great equipment, or even a jersey that fit me well. There I was, running around with an oversized, uncomfortable uniform flopping in the wind. I mean I know I am small, but they could have at least prepared something reasonable for me to wear—I was a signee. They couldn't order a medium or a small? This annoyed me.

After I nailed the 110s, it seemed that nothing went right that first week. I was really down to be honest; I felt bitter every day, filled with disappointment. I wasn't where I wanted to be. I wasn't performing on the level I wanted to be performing. I even ended up getting in a big argument with two of the upper-class linemen in the cafeteria. That night I called my head coach from high school, John Timmons.

I vividly remember telling Coach Timmons how I felt, both physically and mentally. Uncharacteristically, I was dropping balls in camp, I felt slow, and I simply wasn't performing well. "Look, why do you think you were successful in high school?" Coach Timmons asked. "Because you had fun at practice and had fun in the games." That made a lot of sense to me, because since I'd started college, I had not been having fun. My frustration led to dropped passes, missed assignments, and other problems, whereas I had never once dropped the ball in a high school football game. From that point I thought to myself, "Look, if I'm going to be here, I am not going to quit. I'm going to be committed, and I'm going to go out and just have fun."

I woke up the next morning with the attitude that I was going to have fun, and that I was going to dominate. This is when I learned that self-confidence was the only way I was going to make it. From then on, I started taking over in practice and crushing the defensive backs in the "one on ones." A one on one is when the receiver goes against the cornerback with no one else on the field. You have a predetermined route, and the corner has to use man-based techniques to cover you. I dominated in most of the drills, completely taking over now as a freshman receiver.

The momentum was quickly shifting in my favor, as this was the point when the depth chart was starting to take shape for the upcoming season. Doing well in sports has a lot to do with momentum. My goal at this point was to keep this momentum rolling.

In the second week of camp, I figured I had to do something bold to stand out and get the coaches' attention. I called out our best senior cornerback, Brandon Flowers, to cover me one-on-one in front of the whole team, and I ended up winning. I consider this another big turning point in the way the coaches viewed me.

After the first two weeks, I noticed something strange. A lot of the new freshman players were quitting. I didn't know if it was because of the school, the coaching staff, or their position on the depth chart, but players were definitely quitting.

Because of my early experience playing baseball, quitting was hard for me to understand. I had to finish what I started. I learned not to give up because things got too hard, because things didn't go my way, or when I was tired of an activity. In my opinion—to this day—quitters are just losers.

I'd made a complete turnaround on the field, and I was adjusting to college life at Jacksonville University. Things were really rocking and rolling for me. Now, I did have some good competition at receiver, especially from some of the older players, but I was playing with confidence.

At the end of camp, I was already planning on playing because of my position on the depth chart. To my dismay, the receivers' coach pulled me and one of the other receivers, Chad Oubre, to the side. The receiver coach informed us that they were going to redshirt me and play him. We were both in shock after hearing the news. I felt I had outplayed him in camp. Chad, of course, was excited.

The coach said, "Chad is going to play because he is older and has more experience." He wanted me to take the year to learn the game. I was really frustrated and annoyed at going from the possibility of starting receiver to redshirting my freshmen year. Really? Why such a swing? I'll never know the real reason behind it. Did they think I couldn't do it?

Coaches say things to keep players motivated. For example, "You are younger and we wanted to prep you to have four years of domination." It's their job to motivate you, especially if you're on the practice squad.

Even though I redshirted at Jacksonville University, I got much better during the season on the practice squad. I decided that I was here, I was going to have fun this year, and I would use the practice squad as an opportunity to perfect my craft as a receiver. I wanted to learn how to run crisp routes and how to beat man coverage even better on the college level. On the practice squad, I picked up a lot of good habits. I never missed practice and I always played hard.

Halfway through the year, my best friend Dean ended up transferring to another university in Jacksonville, Florida. No longer playing football, he was off scholarship. Going to a private school was just out of the question financially.

Jacksonville was a small college and felt more like high school rather than a university. There were only two thousand students in the school, and everyone knew everyone. Classes were similar to those from high school, and it wasn't the kind of college experience either of us wanted to have, so I didn't blame him for transferring. When he transferred, things became even worse. I was able to hang out on the weekends because I had my car, but the weeks consisted of boring classes, few friends, and practice squad.

That off-season, the training was rigorous, and I ended up gaining plenty of muscle. I was eating a lot, because I felt I needed to gain a lot of muscle and get big. My off-season squat was 400 pounds and I was benching 275 as a freshman, even though I was only five feet seven and weighed 170 pounds. As strong as I was, the extra weight and muscle were simply too heavy for my frame. I didn't realize this until I ran my slowest 40, at 4.8 seconds. I was in shock. One of the other receivers on the team even joked with me, saying I had run a "4-ever."

I mean I packed on some muscle and weight, but I didn't think it would slow me down as much as it did. From a high 4.5-second 40 to a 4.8-second 40. If you don't know 40 times, this is a huge difference. For example, in the NFL, the difference between a 4.49 and a 4.50 could make the difference of being drafted and making millions of dollars.

The coach and the staff that signed me as a freshmen were fired in the off-season. They hired a new coach, Kerwin Bell. Kerwin Bell had an excellent record as a high school coach, as a quarterback at the University of Florida, and in the NFL. The new coaches came in and made dramatic changes—and it was a good thing for the university. The university, in fact, wanted to support the program more. After hiring Kerwin, the school purchased uniforms, upgraded some of the facilities, and strengthened its commitment to football. In general, the school made the right move, but in terms of my football career, it just pushed me back in no man's land.

Everything I showed the coaches in camp and during the season on the practice squad was history. I had to prove myself all over again, and unfortunately, I didn't have a very good spring at all. I feel the reason was because I had gained too much muscle and was too big for my frame. With both the weight and muscle slowing me down, I ended up pulling a quad during the first week of practice. It wasn't a very productive spring in my opinion, and I didn't impress the coaches.

The new coaches were focused on bringing in their own players for the following year. At the end of spring practice, there was always an internal scrimmage. While played only among our own players, it gave the coaches a chance to see the players perform at live game speed. I played very well in this game despite my injury and poor practice. I didn't get much playing time, but I ended up with three big catches. Spring practices ended, and I decided that that summer I was going to drop down in weight and work on nothing but getting my speed back.

That summer I didn't go out at all. I hung out with my girlfriend when I wasn't training, but I never went out or partied. I spent my time training, eating, and watching movies. I did fourteen weeks of four-day-a-week lift and four-day-a-week run, and when I was running, I used "Strength Shoes." These special, strange-looking shoes have no heel, so they make you run on your toes. My workout partner, Eddie Brown, who would later go on to play football at Colgate University, and I both had the strength shoes. You can learn more about these shoes at www.EarnaScholarship.com/StrengthShoes. By the end of the summer we were able to run twenty-four 110s under fourteen seconds with a forty-five-second rest, which was pretty awesome.

That was the hardest three-month training regimen that Eddie and I had ever gone through in our lives, but by the end of that training, we were in terrific shape, and I felt like a bullet. At the very end of the summer, two weeks before I was headed back to Jacksonville University for camp, I received a call from my new receivers' coach, who said, "The numbers aren't looking good, so we're not going to be able to bring you back for camp this year. We'd like you to come back when school starts." What that basically meant was: you didn't have a good spring, and we don't think you're good enough to play during the year, and you're one hundred percent going to be on the practice squad.

They didn't think I was good enough to compete with the older receivers, whom I'd beaten out the year before, nor with the new receivers were they bringing in. After the vigorous summer training, I was pretty down; I remember I was driving in my car at the time of the call, and that I just started crying. When you put in the type of work I did—without direction, with pure self-discipline—something like this can be very disappointing. I called my dad while driving and told him what happened. I couldn't control my emotions. Tears poured down my face.

After the call, I decided that it was over at Jacksonville University. I had about two weeks to figure out what to do, but with the new coaching staff doing what they were to all the players recruited the year before, there was no way I was going back. I wasn't a good fit with the school, the location, or the football program. Being there hadn't been my goal or what I wanted. I proceeded to make a spreadsheet with every D1 school that originally recruited me, and I went to their websites. I found the school phone numbers and coaches' names. I added them to the spreadsheet, printed it out, and began making calls to these coaches to see if they had a walk-on spot for me. After three days of making calls, I had no luck. I didn't even know what cold calling was at the time, but I was doing it. The coaches were nice and would try to help, but once they asked me my height and weight, the conversations ended pretty abruptly. Then finally it hit me. Kyle Strongin!

CHAPTER 3

Disappointment and New Opportunities

I REMEMBERED HEARING FROM A GOOD FRIEND, that our high school offense football coach, Kyle Strongin, had just been promoted to the Operations Manager at the University of Mississippi, better known as Ole Miss. It's funny how things happen in life.

I had met Kyle when I was twelve years old, only a few months after my surgery for a separated and fractured elbow. After surgery, my arm was very weak. When I finally was able to take off the cast, my arm was weak and small, about half the size it had been. After two months of recovery, my dad suggested that I work with a personal trainer to rehabilitate my arm.

My dad signed me up at the gym where he had been going to for years. Before my surgery, I had never worked out a day in my life. I was hitting harder than most of the other kids, and my attitude was "Why do I need a gym when I'm hitting and playing so hard?" Luckily, I did understand my arm was really weak and that I needed to rehab it back to its original strength.

When my dad and I walked into the gym, we explained to the manager the condition of my arm and our desire for a trainer. He said, "I have just the guy for you, hold on." The manager walked out of the room and came back with this tall, model-looking, musclebound man. He was huge! Here I am, this little guy, and Kyle was about six feet three and 240 pounds of pure muscle. Immediately, he had my attention. I was motivated to begin working out right then and there. I wanted to put on some size and be like Kyle.

Kyle was a very smart guy as well. The manager knew he was the right fit; he had just returned from playing football at the University of Oklahoma (OU) with Bob Stoops. Here is the ironic part: Kyle was a walk on. Although he hadn't earned a scholarship, he had some big-time accomplishments there. After I had followed his workout for the first couple of weeks, not only did we begin building a strong relationship but I improved my strength substantially as well. I trained extremely hard with him—three days a week of grinding—and the weight I was lifting consistently went up. At the time, it was a lot for me, but

Kyle instilled in me the techniques and skills I still use today. I remember him being very pleased with my progress. After three months of working out with Kyle, I was ready for high school and began working out with my peers. I missed working out with Kyle, but I was moving on to the scheduled lifts required for the freshman football players at Wellington High School.

After my freshman year, the school boundaries changed, and I was off to Palm Beach Central. During my senior year of high school, Kyle was back in my life. Initially, I saw Kyle speaking to the head coach in the weight room but didn't make the connection right away—the last time I had seen him, I'd been twelve years old. They were drawing plays on the board. I walked by Kyle and he said, "Richie, hey, do you remember me?" Once he said that, I remembered him right away and told him, "Yeah, we trained after I broke my arm." He told me, "Yes, and I'm going to be the new quarterbacks' coach here." Wow! I was excited.

I knew his history of playing in college, and before that as a star high school football player. I looked forward to working with him again and having a young, smart, energetic coach help out our quarterbacks. Getting into coaching, he made a good transition from personal training, and he had good timing. During my senior year, I worked tirelessly to lead the team by example as a captain and a playmaker, and by being the hardest worker on the team. Kyle saw my drive, my character, and the type of player I wanted to be.

During camp, Kyle actually got into it with our starting quarterback. After a few minutes, the quarterback ran off the field right in the middle of practice. His actions were uncalled for, I see looking back, and the team agreed and supported Kyle's position. I ran off and spoke with our quarterback, who ended up returning to practice and apologizing to Kyle.

That had been when Kyle and I had really built a bond. It had also been one of my defining moments of becoming a leader.

After getting the bad news from Jacksonville University, I felt confident about calling Kyle. I told him that I wasn't invited to camp at JU and explained the whole story. He was in shock. He immediately said to me, "Richie, why don't you come play here at Ole Miss?"

I had never imagined it would happen that way; my heart began racing. I started pacing outside in my driveway with excitement. Right away I asked, "What would it take for me to get into Ole Miss?"

He didn't hesitate. He said, "I will do what I can to get you in here." I probably thanked him more than a thousand times as I quietly jumped up and down.

Out of breath, I said, "What do I need to do now? What can I do to make this happen today? Anything you need me to do, I will do right away." His first question was "How are your grades? Can we get you in academically?" Thank god I studied and got good grades. I told him "Yes!"

Next he asked, "Okay, can you get me some tape?" and again I told him yes. He continued, "Let's start with that. Send me your transcripts and your tape. After I speak with the coaches, you need to get released from Jacksonville." Then he explained the full process of transferring. He told me not to do anything except send my transcripts and tape. Kyle wanted to find out how many spots were available and what options he had for me. He didn't want me to quit at Jacksonville University until he was able to pass the first couple steps at Ole Miss and secure a spot.

I sprinted home full speed and told my dad, "I just talked to Coach Strongin!" My dad remembered Kyle well. I told my dad I had an opportunity to get into Ole Miss, one of the most prestigious universities in the country, and, most importantly, to play in the SEC. The SEC West—one of the best football conferences in college football.

Standing in my dad's office, I was breathing heavily in my excitement, and he simply asked, "So what needs to happen?" I let him in on everything I'd discussed with Kyle, and he said, "So, you're telling me the stars have to align?" And I said, "Yes, the stars definitely have to align, but it's possible." I knew that there was an opportunity there, but so many things had to happen in sequence that it was really hard to believe it could happen. Still, in my mind, there was no doubt: I was going to be an Ole Miss Rebel. Call it fate or karma, but I knew I was going to make it all work out, and I was going to be there by the time official practice started.

We sat down and I wrote out the list of everything that needed to be done:

Step one: Get into Ole Miss academically—and the university was way past the transfer deadline at this time.

Step two: Get in some practice tape.

Step three: Secure a spot or a tryout for the team.

Step four: Get released from Jacksonville University.

Step five: Find a place to live.

So, as you can see, the stars really did have to align, and a lot of the deadlines had already passed, including the one for my release from Jacksonville, and for securing a spot and getting into Ole Miss academically. The most important thing was that I needed to get into Ole Miss academically. Fortunately, I had worked really hard in the classroom at Jacksonville University and had good grades, but at this point, we knew nothing was for sure, especially since it was past the transfer deadline.

The next day, I was on the phone with Jacksonville University asking about my transcripts. Kyle was awesome throughout the process. The next day he was in the admissions office trying to find out if he could squeeze me in. I had to run around like crazy between my mom's work and home, because I didn't have a fax machine. It was a wild three days of getting and sending faxes and e-mails and trying to get everything set up. Since it was past the deadline, my grades at Jacksonville had to have been really good. Without the grades at Jacksonville, I wouldn't have had a chance of getting in.

After I'd sent everything I could to Kyle, it was basically a waiting game. I didn't hear back for a while, and Kyle was very busy with the season approaching, so he couldn't just sit in admissions every day and keep pushing them. I was texting him almost daily.

While I felt bad about that, I was strongly motivated to get in, and my persistence was taking over. He was also running around talking to the coaches and trying to get me a spot on the team and a place in camp, but at the end of the day, it was a numbers game.

I knew the next step was finding a place to live. So while I waited, I called pretty much every apartment complex in close proximity to the school, and I found a place that was open and right by the campus. I reserved it immediately, even before I knew I had a place at Ole Miss, wanting to ensure I had that step taken care of. If I lost the down payment, I lost it, but I wasn't going to risk not having a place to live.

Every afternoon around one o'clock, when the mailman came, I was there waiting for my acceptance letter. Finally, I received a call from the admissions office at Ole Miss. My heart was racing. The only one home, I stood at the island in the kitchen of my house. I took a deep breath and said, "Yes, this is Richie." She started out by saying "Congratulations," and I immediately felt a tear roll down my face. I got in! I said thank you over and over again. She laughed because she hadn't even had the chance to finish her sentence. Even past the deadline, Kyle Strongin had made it happen with admissions. I immediately called my mom and my dad and told them. Their excitement was evident but nowhere near my own. I had so much adrenaline in my system, I went outside and ran a lap around my block.

I called Kyle and thanked him over and over again as well. He said, "Congratulations Richie, you deserve it." He'd also just received the news that he was not able to get me into training camp, but he was able to get me a tryout. The fact that I was not in camp didn't even faze me. I looked at getting into training camp as just a plus at this point. I proceeded to thank him over and over again until I couldn't thank him anymore without annoying him.

The last thing that I needed to do was to get released from Jacksonville. I knew that this was going to be a tough thing to do. I talked with my dad about it, and he said, "You know what, I don't think you should call your coach. I think we should go in person and ask for the release." I agreed with him.

Jacksonville University is located in Jacksonville, Florida, a four-hour drive from my house in West Palm Beach, Florida. I called my new receivers' coach from Jacksonville University, Ernie Mills, and said that I would like to meet with him to discuss the upcoming football season. He agreed to meet me, and the next day, my dad and I drove to Jacksonville. We met my coach in the parking lot and he said to me, "Wow, you look good. Looks like you have been training hard this summer." I nodded and said, "Yep, trained pretty hard." There is no way he could have imagined the rigorous training I'd gone through that summer.

We sat in the head coach's office, and I just flat-out said that I wanted a release from the team. He immediately said, "Wait, let me work the numbers . . . I think we can find a spot for you in camp, hold on a minute." Before he could make a move, I told him, "I'm not coming back to Jacksonville University. Please just provide me with a release."

He said, "Whoa, I'm sorry to hear that. Why?"

Nicely, I explained, "Jacksonville University is just not the right place for me." I was really frustrated at the time, because I didn't get invited to camp and I was just another number. A new coach with a new system and new recruits—why did they need me? I guess they would rather take a chance on a new recruit, and if he didn't do well, I would be eagerly waiting in the wings. Not sure if that was the case, but regardless, I was moving on to bigger and better things.

Coach Bell provided me with the release, and I thanked him for the opportunity to play for him. Even though I was frustrated, I didn't want to burn any bridges. During the car ride home, all I could think about was the tryout. It was my one shot. If I didn't make it, there was a good chance I would be out of football for good, and I loved football with all my heart. Leaving JU was a great risk, but in my opinion, it was worth the possible reward. I truly believed in myself, and I knew I could play at Ole Miss. I wasn't afraid; I was excited.

When I got home, I packed my car and then I left for Oxford, Mississippi, with absolutely no regrets. My mom thought it was crazy how everything worked out. One day I had told her, "Hey, I'm going to Ole Miss"—this before everything had come together—and she'd just said, "Make it happen." Then, about ten days later, my car was packed and I was on my way. She brings this up even now, telling me that it was very inspirational for her. If anyone believed in me, it was her, but I can see how my plan would have sounded a bit farfetched. The bottom line was I said that I was going to Ole Miss, and we made it happen. The stars really can align if you believe—they did for me!

My girlfriend accompanied me to Oxford, Mississippi, which was about a fifteen-hour trip from West Palm Beach. Off we went, encountering our first setback when I was pulled over in northern Florida, right before we crossed into Georgia, for tinted windows. After running my license and registration, the policeman said my license was suspended. I had no clue! My dreams of arriving in Oxford were on hold, I was missing my only tryout, and my stress level was going through the roof. On top of everything, the police officer suspected that I might be kidnapping my girlfriend, Kristin. He told her to get out of the car and asked her a bunch of questions. Was this really happening to me?

After the officer finally got to the bottom of the situation and realized I was not a kidnapper, he told me my license was suspended from a previous ticket I didn't pay. I told the officer I had paid my last ticket, and thankfully he believed me. This incident was back before smartphones made it possible to instantly pull up your personal information.

After the police officer took the time to make a few phone calls, he found out that the ticket was paid. Unfortunately, I couldn't drive to Ole Miss just yet, because at the end of the day, my license was technically suspended. The cop instructed me that the next day I had to go to the DMV and get a new license. This was ridiculous. It was only about two o'clock in the afternoon, and we had to delay our drive until the next day. Plus, I was not allowed to drive the car to the hotel. Thankfully, I had Kristin with me, but unfortunately she did not know how to drive stick shift.

When the police officer went back into his car, I had to give her verbal instructions on how to drive a stick shift so we could actually leave. She was under some serious pressure, but she stayed calm and was able to get the car on the highway. I was impressed. We pulled into a hotel right off the highway and right next to the DMV. We made it there safely. What a fiasco!

I needed to be at Ole Miss in two days, and we couldn't leave. This certainly turned up the pressure a couple notches. We had to get a hotel room and wait in Florida until 8:00 a.m. the next day to get my new driver's license. We stayed in the hotel, woke up early, and ran to the DMV at 7:30 so we could be first in line. I filled out the paperwork and got the license. We now had one day to bolt to Oxford. School was starting, and I needed to be rested and ready to roll for my tryout.

High-tailing it, we got to Oxford about 5:45 p.m. The management office of the apartment complex where I was moving closed at six; we made it just in time. The management office told me that I couldn't pay for the first month's rent with a regular check—I needed a cashier's check. Wow. It never ended! I needed the stars to align again for me.

After racing around, I found a gas station nearby that provided cashier's checks. The office administrator was really nice and waited for me to come back with it. That night I was finally able to get into the apartment. The next day, I set up my new apartment and got acclimated to life in Oxford.

The neighborhood I moved into was called Campus Walk. There was a back entrance where you could walk to the university.

I went through there just to take a look at the scenery, and I ended up warming up. I ran eight 110s back there, just to get my breath back and make sure my conditioning was good to go. It felt good because the last couple of days I had been travelling, packing, and dealing with some crazy situations, so I just wanted to work out some stress and give myself a quick conditioning test. I felt I was ready.

Later in the evening, Kristin and I drove around the campus at Ole Miss. The stadium was breathtaking! What a difference between the small private school Jacksonville University and this immaculate Southeastern Conference campus, which was just . . . unbelievable. I was filled with so much joy, but I also was very nervous about the next day.

My first impression of the Ole Miss campus was exactly what I wanted in a college experience. It was really clean, and most people were wearing the Ole Miss team apparel. Jacksonville was a small school, and many of the students had worn apparel from the teams of other, bigger colleges. Where was the team spirit?

At Ole Miss, there was a lot of team spirit, people proudly wearing the Ole Miss Rebels' colors. The love everyone had for the team and university was one of the first things I noticed. You could just feel it. The campus was just amazing—so much tradition, so many statues, and so much meaning to the school.

I'll never forget that initial drive around the campus; I was driving along Manning Way, which is named after Archie Manning. He is the all-time greatest quarterback in Ole Miss history and also had an outstanding career in the NFL. His football jersey number was eighteen, which was also the speed limit on Manning Way. College football is all about tradition.

After the drive, I took my girlfriend to the Memphis airport so she could fly back home to West Palm Beach. She was going to college in Jacksonville. After I got back, I remember sitting down at the kitchen table the night before my first day of class. I had a map of the school and was planning out everything: where I would park, where my first class was, and how I was going to get from class to class.

I tried to go to bed early, but there was no way I was sleeping. I was so excited to be a part of the Ole Miss Rebel family. Finally, I was there, I was going to attend class, and most of all, I had an opportunity to play Rebel football. It was an unbelievable feeling, an unbelievable experience.

I lay in bed that night thinking to myself, "The stars really did align." Some people may call this luck, but my dad always told me, "The definition of luck is when opportunity meets preparedness." I had prepared that whole summer, and opportunity came my way. Coming into my first season at Ole Miss, I was prepared. I had trained and worked so hard that I was confident and believed I could play at Ole Miss. My preparedness embraced the opportunity, and it happened. It was a dream and yet it was real.

CHAPTER 4

One Shot

I DIDN'T GET MUCH SLEEP the night before my tryout. I woke up every hour on the hour and got up way earlier than I needed to. I had a great breakfast and then drove to the planned parking spot, the one I'd picked out the night before. It made it easy to get to my classes and then to football afterward. I was there so early that I was the third car in the entire parking lot. In my first class, there were about three hundred kids in a gigantic auditorium. I was physically there, but I wasn't thinking about the class. I was thinking only, "This is my dream come true. I'm in a college town, in a prestigious university, with an opportunity to play big-time SEC college football." That whole day, I walked from class to class with the biggest smile.

In between classes I had a break, so I met up with Kyle to take a tour of the football facilities. The first thing we did was walk into the indoor practice field (IPF). It was unbelievable! A huge, indoor arena with a full-sized football field. Surrounding the football field was a full-sized track and various workout equipment stations. I was in awe of this extremely cool sight. On the right-hand side of the facility, there was a glass wall that contained the coaches' offices and all the meeting rooms. They designed the facility so all position coaches had an opportunity to view the field from their own offices.

The players' lounge was the first room we visited on our tour. As you walk in to the players' lounge, you see one wall with a list of all the Ole Miss players who went on to play in the NFL. I called it the "Wall of Fame."

The lounge was modern and comfortable, with couches and lounge chairs, and all around the outside edges were flat-screen TVs with PlayStation 3s and Xboxes. In the middle of the room was a computer lab with modern computers and printers. I couldn't believe it. This was the players' lounge? Wow! It was truly unbelievable. We walked into another area that had a pool table, ping pong table, and some arcade games. I said to Kyle, "You have got to be kidding me." He started laughing and said, "Welcome to paradise, my friend."

Next door to the players' lounge was the weight room. This mammoth room had the bench press, squat, and power lifting racks neatly arranged in a perfect line down the middle. All the dumbbells and cardio machines were around the perimeter, neatly arranged.

It had everything you wanted and could imagine in a gym. It was structured perfectly for football. Players were placed in groups by position and strength. The team lifted in sync so the coaches could view individual players and ensure everyone was working hard and, more importantly, improving every day.

The facility always looked brand new and in perfect condition. Included in the amenities were Gatorade and healthy-snack bars. You could go up to the self-serve and pour unlimited amounts of Gatorade. Picture yourself walking into 7-11 and going to the fountain drinks, except it was all Gatorade. Right next to the Gatorade bar was the healthy-snack bar, which contained nuts, protein bars, and all the protein shakes you can imagine. And, yes, it was unlimited and free.

Shock and awe! The facility was something that you would see in a movie or, more accurately, in your wildest dreams. Even some of the nicest gyms I went to didn't have the level of equipment at Ole Miss. It was purely designed for athletes and football explosion muscle building.

The next place we visited was the equipment room. At first, seeing only a few helmets and minor equipment, I thought the room looked small, but as we walked to the back of the room, Kyle opened a door, and I thought I was at the Nike factory. Neatly arranged stacks and rows of assorted shoes, shoulder pads, helmets, gear, and other sports-related equipment. I had no idea the magnitude of the building. I felt as though I was looking into a mirror, because the rows seemed never ending.

We then visited the locker room. Not only was it carpeted and spotless but it smelled good as well. On the walls were Ole Miss jerseys, pictures, and memorabilia from past teams. Flat-screen televisions and a top-notch sound system were in view from every locker. The difference between this locker room and the dampness, smell, hard concrete floors, and small lockers I had grown accustomed to was night and day. The Ole Miss locker room was comparable to any NFL locker rooms you see on television.

Next to the locker room was the training room, which looked like an actual hospital rehab center with multiple examination tables, weights, blow-up balls, stretching rollers, hot tubs, and cold tubs, along with a pool for running. The running pool is an underwater treadmill used for players who can't put pressure on their legs. It's pretty cool how it works. The floor rises up out of the water, you step on to the floor, and the floor then lowers back into the water. When fully submerged, the floor begins moving just like a treadmill. When we walked into the training room, one of the track stars was using it. He had torn his ACL and was trying to stay in shape. I didn't even know such a machine existed.

Our next stop was the coaches' offices. The coach for each position had his own office, with an attached meeting room for player meetings and instruction. Each meeting room had classroom desks, a very large screen, a projector for watching film, and whiteboards for instruction. It was an efficient and effective design for teaching and learning the game of football. I was introduced and shook hands with most of the coaches, including the receivers' coach, Hugh Freeze, who is now the head coach at Ole Miss.

I got the impression that Hugh didn't think I was a player. When Kyle introduced me, he said, "Oh, okay, okay!" He was looking me up and down, all five feet seven inches of me, and probably saying in his head, "You're going to have a long road here. Best of luck, buddy." Hugh was really nice to me, though, saying, "Welcome to the team, we are glad to have you." That made me feel welcome. Coach Freeze then asked Kyle about another walk-on receiver who was supposed to come in, which just made me smile and think, "Okay, the long road begins right now." Throughout my football career, I've become accustomed to one thing: it's hard for a coach to look at my size and get excited.

After visiting the coaches' offices, we began walking through a long underground tunnel leading to the stadium. The tunnel walls were full of pictures, stats of players who are now in the NFL, and graphic images of the team during games. The graphic design was impressive. I called it the "Walk of Fame."

At the end of the tunnel are double doors that lead you under the stadium seats. The walkway becomes narrow just before you enter the field, and there lies a bust of Chucky Mullins. Chucky was an inspirational defensive back who played at Ole Miss. He was known for his hard work, resilience, and dedication to the team. Unfortunately, Chucky sustained a debilitating football injury that left him paralyzed. Chucky's determination and will to live continues to inspire the Ole Miss family even after his untimely death.

Every year there is a preseason banquet honoring Chucky. The banquet is highlighted by an awards ceremony recognizing the best defensive player and leader with the attributes and positive spirit of Chucky. The recipient of the award has the honor of wearing Chucky's number, thirty-eight.

Once you walk past the statue of Chucky Mullins, you transition onto the turf and get your first glimpse of the entire stadium. And the first thing I did was take a full 360-degree view of it. It was breathtaking! I immediately imagined running out of the tunnel, jumping up and down, and getting the crowd ready for a big game. Even with no one in the stands, I could feel the energy. I had never truly walked out of the tunnel of a stadium before, and I was overwhelmed. I was relieved to feel so at home. I just stood in awe and took it all in. This was going to be my home, my stadium, and my field.

After the tour, Kyle and I walked back through the tunnel to the indoor practice facility. I thanked him again for everything he had done for me before heading off to lunch and my final class of the afternoon. I was still walking around with a huge smile on my face.

On a side note, the women at Ole Miss were beautiful with so much school spirit and passion, proud to be Rebels. It was walking around in heaven. The campus, the women, the football facilities . . . I knew I'd worked really, really hard to get here, but still, having an opportunity to even try out for the practice squad was a dream come true. There was no way anyone was taking this dream from me. I was determined to dominate this tryout and failure was not an option.

Walking back to the practice facilities for the tryout, I had some serious butterflies in my stomach. I didn't know what to expect. It was getting close to the beginning of pre-practice meetings for all of the position players on the roster and also the players who were invited to camp. There I was among the elite Ole Miss SEC players, and I thought to myself, "Holy smokes!" I'd just seen Michael Orr, Mike Wallace, Dexter McCluster, and Greg Hardy walk into their meetings. Wow, what an introduction to the SEC. What a cool first experience.

All I brought to the tryout were my cleats, my desire, and my determination to make this team. I knew the conditioning test was going to be difficult, but I was ready for anything. I got to the IPF early and warmed up on my own. I remember some of players walking by looking at me as if to say, "Who is this guy and why is he out here warming up with us?" I imagine they knew that there was a tryout.

I tried not to look at the players, but it felt as though they were staring right at me. I wasn't sure if they were laughing at me or if their laughter was confined to their own conversation, but, regardless, nothing was getting in my way today. I was confident that after they saw me play, the only thing they would be laughing at was the defender in front of me.

About ten minutes later, everyone had arrived. The conditioning coach came in and tried to intimidate us by saying, "This is going to be extremely difficult, and if this isn't something that you truly want, you should walk away now." This was the first and only warning for players who were not serious. These coaches were SEC-serious and didn't want to waste their time. No one walked away.

The conditioning coach then proceeded to tell us about the conditioning test: We needed to run sixteen 110s with a forty-five-second rest, and we had fourteen seconds to run them. We warmed up as a group—there were about fifteen of us. I'm glad we had the opportunity to warm up because doing so settled the butterflies inside my stomach. Kyle walked out as we finished, and I knew I couldn't let him down. I had been conditioning for this over the summer. I knew I was ready because three weeks earlier, I had run twenty-four 110s at my peak. It was finally time to begin the test.

The high-energy conditioning coach yelled, "Everyone on the line! Ready, go!" I remember when I accelerated out for the first one, I was in the very front. I remember thinking, "You've got to slow down, you've got to relax, because you're going to burn yourself out." My adrenaline was pumping so hard that I had difficulty containing my energy. The first three 110s were a breeze. I started getting tired at number four, and I knew I just needed to relax and stay focused. I did notice that everyone around me was also getting tired as well. This was about the point where your natural adrenaline begins to diminish and people who aren't in shape begin showing fatigue.

Three of the others were also in very good shape. We ran neck and neck on every rep, not breathing hard. At rep eight or nine, I noticed several people had dropped off. I was surprised that people came to the conditioning test unprepared and began dropping off about halfway through the drill—on the floor and as spent as if it was their first time. They had the opportunity of a lifetime, they weren't prepared, and they failed and quit! Really? It was hard to believe. This is when it occurred to me that not everyone is prepared to do the hard work to be successful.

When guys started dropping off, I really got pumped and motivated. Being in the front on every rep and watching people drop off actually makes it even easier to run the final 110s. At rep ten, I caught my second wind. Bam! The afterburners kicked in with a whole new burst of energy. There was nothing stopping me now. I was in the front row competing with one other guy, and it was on. We were battling to be first on every single rep. I was tired, but I was also in shape. I believe that when you're in shape, you're still going to be tired after each rep, but being in shape accelerates your recovery.

During those final reps, a calm came over me that dispelled my nervousness completely. I felt good and was growing more excited. I tossed my shirt before running the last couple reps. I finished. I'd prepared, and I did it. What a sense of accomplishment—and relief. Next were the position drills.

I felt the position drills were my strength. I knew that once we cycled through the drills, it was a wrap. All the extra practice, playing "bushes" in the front yard with Zach, and working hard culminating into my mastery of position drills. We ran through the complete wide receiver route tree. I didn't drop the ball once, and I was consistently in the front, the first person to go in every drill. I didn't even feel tired. I wanted this and I was so close.

At the end of the tryout, we were told that we would get a call that night informing us if we made the team. I went home and ate dinner, trying to just relax. Focusing on anything except the tryout was impossible though. When was the call coming? What was the outcome? Had I made the team?

As I was getting everything ready for the following day—organizing and reorganizing my books, papers, schedule—the phone rang, and it was Kyle. He was laughing. I was said, "What? What?" He said, "Hey Richie, guess what? You made the practice squad. Congratulations." I was speechless. I couldn't even say a word. He said, "Hello?" I composed myself enough to say, "I'm here Kyle, thank you so much for everything." I was surprisingly calm, relieved, and full of faith. My ego didn't want it to seem to Kyle that I was shocked; I wanted him to believe I'd known I had it in the bag. I had crushed the conditioning test and done well on the position drills. I mean, why wouldn't I make the team right? Wrong.

My size, five feet seven, is a killer when it comes to competing for a roster spot on the varsity team, but that's not the case for making the practice squad. Kyle went on to say, "But I just want to let you know exactly how this works and what you're in for." He was referring to the expectations of the practice squad, so I was one hundred percent aware and prepared.

Kyle explained that on the practice squad, I was going to wear a black jersey at practice while the regular starters split the jersey colors. For example, offensive players wore blue jerseys and defensive players wore white. The QBs and the injured players wore red. He said, "Be prepared to be the hitting dummy for the starters and backups. I know you are a good player, but you must put your ego aside and give your body to the team. This is your only chance to make the team. Your job is to run the opposition's plays and prepare the starters for the upcoming weeks."

I replied, "Don't worry Kyle, you know me and I am going to give my all, mind, body, and soul to help this team win games on Saturday. This is my dream and I will sacrifice anything for you and the team, especially after what you have done for me." Lastly, Kyle told me that I would have one week on the field to prove that I should stay on the practice squad and officially be on the Ole Miss roster.

"So I didn't officially make the team yet?" I asked.

He replied, "Not yet. There are some extra guys here and we only want to place the best quality players on the team to represent the university." He assured me, however, "I have all the confidence you're going to make the team—just do what you normally do. Stay the course. The coaches are looking for the top guys to really prove themselves, both on and off the field, and show they deserve to be an Ole Miss Rebel. You deserve it Richie, just take it."

I said, "Yes sir, Kyle! Thank you again for everything." When I hung up the phone, I immediately called my mom and dad, so excited to tell them the news I was laughing. I was ready to crush my first day of D1 SEC football practice the following day; I just needed to find a way to fall asleep.

CHAPTER 5

Just When You Think You Made It

DAY TWO AT OLE MISS, and I was even more excited than on day one. My butterflies were worse and my nerves were going crazy. It was impossible for me to concentrate in class. Going from class to class, all I could think about was the excitement of playing football for Ole Miss in the prestigious SEC. I'd once only dreamed of playing for this program; knowing it was a reality was a great feeling. Again, I parked right next to the practice fields, which were right next to the stadium.

The practice fields were immaculate. Maintenance staff were mowing the grass and painting the lines. Mmmm, the smell of fresh-cut grass. You could just see the care and pride they had when maintaining the fields and doing their part in getting the team ready for post-camp practice. All I could think about that day was getting to the locker room and receiving my pads, jersey, and Ole Miss helmet.

Since I was new, I didn't know the ropes. I wasn't sure if I was going to get a locker, if I was allowed to get my ankles taped, if I was allowed to get a protein shake, or even if I would have a jersey with a number. It was difficult to stay focused during the school day with these questions cycling through my mind. I just didn't know at all what to expect.

I was asked to meet the equipment manager at 3:30 p.m. to receive my practice uniform and gear. At this same time, the starters, second-stringers, and scholarship players were in their skill position meetings. I walked right across the turf practice field to the equipment room. Everybody was running around and speaking quickly, trying to get things done. I felt as though I was in New York City.

When I walked up to the equipment room, the manager immediately said, "What's your name and what's your size?" I asked, "Size for what?" and he replied, "For clothes." I told him my size was a medium. He turned around, grabbed a few pieces of clothing, and tossed them in my direction. He also tossed some shoulder pads over my head and said, "Yup, they fit you." I was able to try on two helmets before my correct size was determined. He then said, "Here is your locker number—thirty-one." Wow. It was fast and efficient, and I had a clear picture of where I stood as a walk-on. Walk-ons are not very high on the totem pole.

Obviously, they were really busy and they were probably used to seeing tons of people like me come and go through the door. Here on the first day and then quitting shortly thereafter. Why spend time with a walk-on? I get it. From there, I walked over to the locker room, and one of the equipment guys noticed that I didn't have a name tag. He pulled out a piece of tape, put it on my locker, wrote my name, and said, "Here you go, this is your spot for the week." Little did he know this was going to be my spot for the next four years!

They segmented the locker room by position, so my area was with all wide receivers. Three of the receivers near my locker— Mike Wallace, Dexter McCluster, and Kendrick Lewis—became starters in the NFL. Kendrick ended up moving to safety, but at the time, he was a wide receiver. I remember Mike Wallace strolling in with McDonald's and being really nice to me. He told me he was "holding the receiver core down." Whatever that meant. He was laughing and I just went with it. I bonded the quickest with Kendrick, who was right across from me and also treated me very well.

A big difference between Ole Miss and Jacksonville University was the confidence level of the receivers. At JU, the older players were not very friendly and tried to intimidate the younger ones. Not at Ole Miss—most players were friendly and supportive, probably because Ole Miss players were very secure in their talents. At JU, I think the insecurities about losing a starting position prevented team relationships from building and growing.

There I was, sitting at my locker waiting for practice to start, watching the starters getting out of their meetings and ready for practice. The select few who made it past the initial tryout went straight into full pads on day one. Yes, you heard that correctly. There were no days of practice without pads. During my entire football life, going back to little league, there had always been a required period of days without pads to get your body acclimated for intense physical contact. I knew the reasoning was to protect players from injury. I found out very quickly that was not the intent regarding the practice squad. We were in full pads with full hitting, from day one. You really see the logic for the vigorous conditioning test. Without the conditioning test, kids could get seriously injured. Especially if you are undersized like me.

There was a schedule on my locker indicating that everyone needed to be on the practice field in twenty minutes. I was changed and ready to go, so I went ahead and walked to the practice field. As I looked around, I thought, "Man, am I the smallest guy out here or what!"

I noticed three fields, and I had no idea where to go, so I just started stretching and waited for other players to walk out from the locker room. As I was stretching, I noticed a group of scholarship players and coaches talking and strategizing. One of the coaches called me over, and within about thirty seconds, I was getting pounded in a drill. He didn't know me and I didn't know him. He wasn't the head coach, just an assistant. He pushed me around, giving the scholarship players a glimpse of possible moves by next week's opposition.

It was hilarious. I was on the field for less than two minutes and I was already getting whipped around like a rag doll. The best part was that I was getting whipped around by a coach, not a player. Welcome to the SEC and the practice squad.

About fifteen minutes before practice started, I saw Head Coach Ed Orgeron running out of the indoor practice facility, screaming and yelling. He was really excited about practice! He was yelling, "Come on, come on!" as he watched people walk out onto the practice field. He was very, very intense. I was standing there saying to myself, "Wow, this guy is motivating." He was ready for practice, that's for sure.

All of us on the practice squad with our black jerseys were known as the "Blackshirts." The regular starters, of course, were wearing the Rebel-blue and -white jerseys. One of the assistant coaches started yelling for all of the practice squad offensive players to get in their places, and I hustled over.

There were about twenty players on the offensive practice squad. The group consisted of players from the recent tryout, red-shirted players, and players who were just not very good.

The coaches began by picking out eleven guys who would run the opposing teams' plays. The first drill was called the "Fit Drill." They picked players they knew, including QB Jevan Sneed and a few other scholarship players. I remember for the receivers, it was just the first people in the huddle. I didn't look around—I just ran into the huddle, stood there, and didn't stay a word. Since

I was in the huddle, the coach tapped me on the helmet to go. Practice began.

We did the Fit Drill every day against the starting defense. Our job was to walk through the plays and help the defensive players work on their alignment. Practice started with a warm-up and stretches, and then we went from zero to sixty running the opposing teams' plays.

The coaches had created and used small poster cards with the opposing teams' offensive plays drawn on them. An assistant coach would hold up a play card, and the offense would take position. There were usually two to five receivers required on a play, so you would call out which receiver you were and run to your position. I took the initiative and ran to a receiver position first. As a result, I was in the first receiver group, ahead of some of the scholarship players. Trust me, that action was noticed quickly during the week. I sprinted on the field and started running the opposing teams' plays. The first day, I had four big catches and I was flying around the defense. It was a blast! The defense wasn't used to someone going full speed every single play. This was my chance to make my mark on the team.

Next in practice we focused on "hitting drills." The coaches made human hitting dummies of us Blackshirts. The play started about twenty feet away from a linebacker. My job was to run the ball at an angle without making any kind of move to juke the linebacker or protect myself. His job was to form tackle me. I was functionally a hitting dummy with no defense for five to ten minutes at every practice. To protect myself, I would actually try to hit them first and tighten all of my muscles. That really made them mad, but it was much better than just trying to absorb the hit and keep getting my butt whipped.

After the human hitting dummy drill, we went back to running the opposition's plays. I took my opportunity to run with the first team, trying to get as many reps as possible. The next segment of practice was called one-on-ones. The one-on-one drill is designed for the starting receivers to go up against the starting defensive backs. The practice squad watched from the sideline. After the one-on-one dill was completed, we went back to "team" until the end of practice. "Team" is when the starting offense goes against the starting defense. The players don't tackle, but they "thud" against each other. "Thud" is when players hit each other and wrap up but you do not tackle to the ground. This is a good way to continue to work on form, stay live, and avoid injuries.

At the very end of this practice, we did intense conditioning. This was my opportunity to stand out, and I made the most of it. With my hard work, there was no doubt in my mind I was getting noticed.

The conditioning began as we took off our helmets and shoulder pads and ran half-gassers. A half-gasser is a drill in which you run from one sideline to the other and then back to where you started. We had to run each half-gasser in less than sixteen seconds, with a forty-five-second rest. We had to run ten half-gassers that day. I was in the top three on every rep, even after practicing full throttle.

The entire week consisted of these intense physical practices, and that's not including meetings, film, or the weight-room training session. The position meetings were held every day before practice for about an hour. These meetings were not mandatory for the Blackshirts, but after that first day, I never missed a meeting. The coaches didn't speak or acknowledge me in the meetings, so naturally I didn't receive any feedback or encouragement—I wasn't a scholarship player, and the coaches were focused on working with the scholarship players—but I also wanted to learn and take the experience all in. I wanted to see firsthand how the coaches ran the meeting and what the players were learning. I felt that understanding the opposing team's strategy could help me be a more knowledgeable and accurate offensive player for the defense.

Besides practice, meetings, and drills, we also had a workout schedule for the weight room. The workout schedule for the Blackshirts, was Monday, Wednesday, and Thursday morning at 6:00 a.m.

At 6:00 a.m. on Thursdays, we had the "crazy workout of the week." I would walk into the weight room at 5:55, and both the strength and conditioning coach would be pumped up and excited to get the workout underway. We hit the gym hard, and after the "official" workout was complete, we would start the crazy competition.

The feats of strength tested were for the most push-ups, or most squats, or whatever the drill the coaches had in mind. At the first Thursday workout, we had a push-up competition—I came in second place. It was tough but exciting. At the end of the day, it was a very solid competition that got all of us wound up.

The starters and scholarship players didn't have a workout on Thursday. They were preparing for the upcoming game and Friday's walk through. I guess you could say "crazy competition Thursday" was our game-day walk through.

Wow, did the week fly by. By Thursday, having finished my first week of practice, man I was beat. I was in the best shape of my life, though. I gave it my all and I made an impact. The workouts, the practice, and the poundings were exhausting, but I didn't care; I was pumped and excited to be part of Ole Miss. The excitement of playing overrode my exhaustion, and nothing fazed me. I was good!

That Thursday night, some of the Blackshirts who weren't traveling went to a popular bar in Oxford called The Library. Going out with the guys from the team was a great bonding experience. The first thing I noticed when we walked into The Library were the amazingly beautiful women. Ole Miss was the college experience I'd longing for, and here I was. That night, we all hung out as teammates, got to know each other, talked with beautiful women, and built some camaraderie. Then back to my apartment for some well-needed rest.

During my first year, I lived in an apartment with three roommates, and I was so busy during the first week I hadn't met any of them until we crossed paths that night. One of my roommates was a former Ole Miss receiver who had graduated a few years earlier. I remember telling him I was a receiver and explaining my story. At first he was in shock—you know, my size again—but he immediately turned it into a positive. He became an important person and mentor that first season. He told me that life gets easier once you're promoted from the practice squad. He said, "Keep fighting and you will eventually get promoted." He was just a very positive influence on me.

The team would eat dinner every day after practice, but only the scholarship athletes were allowed to eat in the dining room. At first I was upset, but not eating with the team ended up being one of the best things that ever happened to me.

I began my quest of studying nutrition, smart grocery shopping, and the zen-like art of eating healthy at Ole Miss. I was passionate about nutrition and started to develop the powerful eating habits I still engage in today. In the beginning, I developed my eating regimen on my own with very little direction. I did know one thing: if I was going to have a chance to compete, I had to learn how to fuel my body with the most nutritious, best tasting, and inexpensive foods possible.

The first game was Saturday and I wasn't traveling with the team. We were playing the University of Memphis, only about an hour drive from Oxford. As a member of the team, I was allowed two free tickets per game, so I asked my girlfriend Kristin to fly up to Memphis for the game. I picked her up from the Memphis Airport and took her to the game. It was awesome. We got there about four hours early to just walk around and take in the experience. I was happy knowing that in less than a year, I would be suiting up in a game like this one.

I had been going up against Dustin Mouzon, one of the defensive backs, all week in practice. Early in the game, Dustin had an interception and returned it for a 100-yard touchdown. I remembered how we had run the play during practice as I watched the replay on the Jumbotron. I also closely watched defensive end Greg Hardy, now an excellent player in the NFL. This game stuck out to me because they put Greg in at receiver on the goal line. Greg jumped over a defensive back and caught a touchdown. It was a great call by the coaches. Ole Miss won.

The stadium was packed, as this was the home opener for Memphis. There must have been fifty-five thousand to sixty thousand people in attendance. I felt really good watching the game, especially during that interception, knowing that I had helped Dustin Mouzon succeed. I wasn't playing on the field, but I knew I'd done my part to help the team win. All I could do was smile.

Week one of practice and the first game was now in the books. We had a great week of practice and we won game one of the season. On Sunday I dropped my girlfriend off at the airport and went back to Oxford to get ready for Monday morning. What a great week! I wanted the season to last forever and was so grateful it was only week one—eleven more games still to play in this young season. I was prepared, in shape, and excited for practice and for the season.

The experience exceeded my expectations in every way. Being a Rebel and playing in the SEC was a dream come true—Saturday was the dream and Monday the reality. Monday morning, I would find out if I'd made the team. Another night of being on edge. Another waiting game.

CHAPTER 6

The Dress List

ON THAT FIRST TRIP TO MEMPHIS, I couldn't have been more pumped about my future at Ole Miss. Although nervous, I had a good feeling that I'd made the team (especially after seeing my competition perform on the scout team). I felt I stood out as one of the hardest workers and, overall, one of the best.

On Monday, I went to school as I would have any other day, but man, I was still stressed out of my mind. I walked nervously to the IPF for practice, praying over and over that I was on the dress list to practice. I knew once I walked through that door, I would see the posted list. Everyone would. My heart raced as I approached the list, but I acted cool, as though I knew I was on it. "Please, I don't want to be embarrassed," I thought.

I opened the door with hands drenched in sweat and then walked confidently, giving off the air that I assumed I had made the list. I casually glanced over and saw Contartesi in bold letters. I smiled gently and continued walking through the door. All the stars had aligned for me again. I was thinking: YES, I MADE IT!

Step 1: I'd made the list. Done. Step 2: I went into the locker room praying that my piece of tape was still on my locker. Yes, done. Step 3: I found out I had a new black jersey to wear for the upcoming week, and it was number nine. How cool, I was going to be playing the role of Jeremy Maclin, one of the best players for Missouri, our next opponent.

This next game was a home game in Oxford. The coaches said the best players on the practice squad would dress for the game. Really? I went from possibly not being on the practice squad to having an opportunity to dress in an SEC home game? Yes! The statement resonated with me: "The best players in practice will get a chance to dress for the Missouri game." Talk about incentive.

As a transfer, I knew I had no shot at all to play in the game. Not only was I on the practice squad, but I'd also transferred from a 1 AA school to a Division 1A school. According to NCAA rules, I was not eligible. I didn't care; just the opportunity to dress was exhilarating. I never imagined that I could be dressing in my second week at Ole Miss, against Missouri, in our home opener.

Missouri was a solid team and always contending for the Big 12 championship. They had the powerhouse tandem of quarterback Chase Daniel and receiver Jeremy Maclin. I was wearing Maclin's number nine this week based on my practice team performance from week one, which in itself was pretty exciting.

During practice, I ran a ton of screen routes, which had been my core competency in high school. Get me the ball in space, please! The coaches wanted the quickest guy on the field to run these routes. The route wasn't as much about speed as about quickness and accuracy. The receiver had to be able to "squeeze around" and get from zero to full speed quickly.

My schedule for the week was intense and exhausting. I had to wake up early for school, attend daily position meetings, and kill it at practice and in the weight room. The routine was more intense and detail-oriented in every aspect than my old one at Jacksonville. There were daily weigh-ins; sign-ins for every activity; training room treatments for aches, pains, and injuries; and equipment options.

Ole Miss knew every aspect of your physical condition. They recorded your exact weight, your body fat percentage, your specific workout routine, the nutrition you consumed after your workout, how long you watched film, how long you practiced, and of course your performance during practice. By capturing and analyzing this data, the coaches were better prepared to make informed decision about a player's health and ability to perform.

It was a daily grind for practice-squad guys. We ran multitudes of the opposition's plays without much rest. We also had those "extra crazy" workouts on Thursday. I know we didn't play with the starters on game day, but practice for Blackshirts and Redshirts was rough. The starters and their direct backups get more rest; it's more of a mental game for them during the week.

The coaching staff was focused on developing the scholarship Blackshirt players for the next season. The practice squad was an endurance test ensuring scholarship players possessed the will and desire to be on the varsity team. The intense workouts and extra reps in practice would either motivate you to succeed or force you to quit and move on

On Thursday of week two, I felt I'd had a great week of practice. I liked Thursday for two reasons. First, it was the final practice day for Blackshirts. Second, and more importantly, this Thursday I was going to find out after practice if I made the dress list for the Missouri home game.

As I began walking off the field, the practice squad coach approached me with a big wad of chewing tobacco in his mouth. He was an aggressive man with a deep raspy voice. It seemed as though he had to scream when speaking to you. He said me emphatically, "You're dressing for the game, but you're not traveling." I wanted to ask him a few questions: What time does the bus leave? Where do I meet the team? But he walked away so fast I didn't have a chance to get in a word.

The stars had aligned for me again. Unbelievable. I was dressing for the home opener! I was so excited, I immediately called mom and dad. I spoke quietly because I didn't want anyone in the locker room to hear my conversation, but I couldn't contain myself. I was pumped with excitement and energy. Here I was in my second week at Ole Miss, and I was dressing for the home opener. Bonus: it was a nationally televised game. I had come a long way since leaving JU.

Missouri

The night before every home game, the team travelled and stayed at a hotel in Tupelo, Mississippi. This ritual was meant to keep the players together and focused on the game. No partying or shenanigans here. Once the team left Oxford on Friday, all focus was on the game. Dependent on the start time of the Saturday's game, the team would usually review game film, watch a movie, eat dinner, and have a brief team meeting, and then it was lights out.

In the morning, there was a short church service and breakfast. After breakfast, the team prepared for the final walk-through before boarding the bus back to Oxford. Next stop was the "Walk of Champions." This is a proud Ole Miss football tradition in which, prior to every home game, the players disembark from the bus, form one long line, and walk on a cement pathway called the "Walk of Champions." It was awesome. The fans cheered us on, high-fived us, and really pumped up the team. The "Walk" proceeds directly through a crowd of thousands of fans right in the heart of tailgate country.

The big party was called "Tailgate in the Grove," and it was insane. Ole Miss is always ranked as one of the top three universities in the country for tailgating, and it was easy to see why. The atmosphere was that of New Year's Eve, Christmas, a wedding, a family reunion, and your birthday all rolled into one. Thousands of fans dressed in Ole Miss attire, partying in tents with plenty of food and drinks. In the Grove, one could see fraternity brothers and sorority sisters wearing suits and dresses.

It was also the first time I saw tents furnished with flat-screen TVs, couches, and, unbelievably, a chandelier hanging right in the middle. I'd never seen anything like it. Oxford was a town of about 26,000 people. On game day, the population expanded to about 130,000. And get this: the Grove was only ten acres. They packed them in like sardines.

Only a handful of us didn't travel to Tupelo, but hey, we were dressing for the game. The coaches told us to meet in front of the athletic dorm rooms. This was about a quarter mile from both the Grove and the Walk of Champions. Once the bus with all of the traveling players arrived, the non-travel guys squeezed in behind the team bus with the travel players and we walked together to the Walk of Champions. The goal for the non-travel guys was to get from the athletic dorm to the buses without too many people seeing you.

The Walk of Champions is worth revisiting. It was a once-in-a-lifetime experience. It took a total of ten minutes to travel from one end of the walk to the other, with fans so close to the edge of the sidewalk we could literally stick out hands and high five with the crowd. When I walked through, I had both hands out slapping high-fives the whole way. To top it off, there was a mosh pit of sorts at the end of the walk. About five fans had kept up the tradition of moshing for years. Picture this: when you get toward the end of the walk, this large group of guys start jumping up and down, and you have to get in and jump up and down with them. It's definitely a fun way to get pumped up for the game.

At first, I didn't know what the heck was going on, but I

watched everyone around me and started doing the same thing. It was a blast. I was laughing the whole time. I wish one of the older guys would have given me a heads up, but hey, what the heck.

After the Grove, we continued to walk directly to the stadium. When the entire team had arrived at the stadium, we walked to the center of the field and huddled. We all put our hands in the huddle, said a prayer, and then shouted—very loudly—"Ole Miss!" We walked as a team in silence back to the locker room. Everyone was now focused on the game and their responsibilities.

When I entered the locker room, a few things immediately made me feel like part of the team. I had an official name tag, for one—no more ripped piece of tape with my name on it. I had a clean, shiny helmet. My jersey was already on my shoulder pads, and my socks and my leg pads were perfectly organized. Lockers were emptied of everything except game attire.

The trainers spent hours preparing the locker room for game day. It was really professional. They even placed two pieces of gum and a copy of the game program in everyone's locker. I thought that was a finishing touch. In one corner of the locker room was a small snack bar and in another corner an equipment bar where you could get wristbands, eye tape, new gloves, and so on. Since I wasn't officially playing, I really didn't need any extra accessories.

When I opened my locker, I was shocked. It contained new cleats, gloves, and everything else I could possibly need for the game. At Jacksonville, I was usually looking for a uniform and equipment that fit me. If I wanted extra or new cleats and gloves, I had to purchase them at Dick's Sporting Goods before the game.

It was the difference between D-1AA and D-1A.

I quickly got dressed, and yes, I snapped some pictures on my phone. I couldn't help it. Hopefully nobody saw me, but I wanted to get as many pictures as possible of my locker, with my name tag, and me in my new uniform. I didn't want to forget this day.

The coaches wrote the game-time itinerary on the whiteboard in the locker room. It had the times that each position group was scheduled for their initial warm-up on the field. I went out on the field to warm up with all of the receivers, including Mike Wallace, Dexter McCluster, and Shay Hodge. It was my first time running out of the tunnel on game day. I knew the stadium was not going to be at capacity, but heck, I was just excited to get on the field. To my surprise, when we ran out of the tunnel, there were actually quite a few people in the stands. They cheered as we ran out on to the field. Running out of the tunnel, I could feel the goosebumps cascade throughout my body.

We began with the basic warm-up, and there wasn't much to it. Just simple ball drills and catching drills. We then moved on to running the shorter routes, at about 80 percent speed. I felt great—warmer and faster than I'd ever felt the field. The excitement and adrenaline had taken over.

After about fifteen minutes with the receiver group, we came back into the tunnel and waited for the other position groups to finish. After all the groups were in the tunnel, we then ran out of the tunnel and warmed up as a team. The goosebumps intensified as I ran out of the tunnel for the second time. I couldn't believe that the stadium was already about halfway full; the game didn't start for another hour. And it was already loud.

The final round of warm-ups started with the receivers running the route tree. It was a little intimidating having the quarterbacks throwing us bullets right in the middle of the field. Only one receiver at a time would run a route, and you could just feel all eyes in the stadium on you. I was okay with that; I was catching every pass and having a blast. Trust me, I wasn't going to mess up this opportunity. I didn't want to be the guy who dropped the ball. Heck, if I dropped one, they may never let me dress again.

After warm-ups, the team went back in the locker room. Coach Orgeron gave us a speech about being 2 and 0, and about taking that next step toward winning the conference championship. Missouri was really a good team at the time. Ole Miss was a young team, but I believed we had the talent to win.

About four minutes before the game, we started walking up the underground hallway from the locker room to the stadium. This was the moment I had been dreaming about since I Pee Wee football. My love and passion for football had culminated in this moment. I was running out of the tunnel in front of sixty thousand screaming fans.

Everyone stayed silent and focused as we walked through the tunnel. The only sounds emanating were the music of our cleats on the floor. We approached the edge of the tunnel and were standing near the apron of the stadium. I could hear the crowd booing the other team as they ran out onto the field. As we began to move onto the apron of the field, the crowd was able to see us.

That's when the volume level increased dramatically. I was in the middle of the pack. Now that the team was assembled, we were ready for game time. Coach Orgeron gave the go sign and we all ran onto the field.

The place went wild. Over sixty thousand screaming fans ready for football, for the season opener. I was experiencing the most overwhelming natural high. I ran out of the tunnel and jumped around to see the whole stadium, making a few 360s to make sure I took in everything. It was unbelievable, better than I had ever imagined.

My muscles didn't feel any stress as I ran on the field; I was gliding. The moment brought me back to my little league football days and Coach Dave. At the time, Coach Dave had told my dad, "Your son is a talented player. I hope one day in the future he gets a chance to play college football and run out of the tunnel with sixty thousand screaming fans." He'd hit it right on the money. It was almost scary that sixty thousand is the number he had named. Coach Dave played at the University of Miami, so he knew what the experience meant to a college football player. Maybe he believed it, or maybe it was an incentive, I don't know, but at a young age, he saw something in me. Thanks Dave!

At every Ole Miss home game, the entire stadium does what's called the "Hotty Toddy" chant. I'd heard fans chanting it at school, at bars, and in the Grove—but sixty thousand chanting in unison! Someone came on the Jumbotron, gave a quick speech, and said, at the end, "Are you ready?" Every fan in the stadium started yelling, "Hell ya, damn right, hotty toddy, gosh almighty, who the hell are we, hey, flim flam, bim bam, Ole Miss by damn." It was nuts. I thought" I really need to learn the chant, like, yesterday.

We ended up losing the game, even though we played well and fought hard. We were just a very young team. The core of the team and most of our best players were sophomores. You had the feeling that because we were so young and played so well, we were going to be dangerous in the upcoming years. Coach Orgeron was only in his third year and was already a master recruiter who had stacked the team with awesome players. Get this: more than eighteen guys on this team went on to play in the NFL.

Vanderbilt

The next game was at Vanderbilt. I knew there was no chance to travel or dress, it being an away game, but I practiced and performed my best all week to help the team. Unfortunately, we lost. After losing to Vanderbilt, I knew practice was going to be a meat grinder. We shouldn't have lost to Vanderbilt. My mom was planning on coming to town the following week for our next home game, against the University of Florida.

Florida

Percy Harvin was Florida's best player, and that's who I emulated during practice. I knew if I was going to have a chance to dress for an SEC game, I was really going to have to go all out every play. I was also going to have to make big plays in practice and really stand out.

On Thursday, I felt confident I would dress. Instead of

waiting for the list to be posted, I asked the coach directly, "Am I dressing?" He looked at me and said, "We can't dress as many guys for the non-conference games, and we need to let all of our scholarship guys dress." He looked at me again and said, "You know what, let me see what I can do."

I was waiting impatiently in the locker room, praying I'd have the chance to dress. Finally, he rushed in the locker room as if he had to be somewhere important. He walked right past me and said, "You're dressing." Yes! I was dressing for the game, and my mom would be in attendance. Finally, I would have the chance to show her what I had been working for.

For the second week, I met the other non-travel players by the dorm and squeezed in with the travel squad as they arrived from Tupelo, Mississippi, on the bus. As I did the Walk of Champions, I saw my mom, and I stopped to give her a hug. She beamed with pride. My mom recognized how a lifetime of sacrifice and hard work had brought me to this point.

We began warming up by positions and then as a team. Here I am, on the same field with all the amazing players from Ole Miss and the University of Florida. It was really exciting. The University of Florida (UF) team had All-SEC players Percy Harvin and Tim Tebow among many others. The game was electric, big plays coming from Ole Miss receivers Dexter McCluster and Mike Wallace. I was running up and down the sidelines screaming in excitement for our team. Anytime they'd stop Percy Harvin on a screen, I felt I had contributed. We almost won the game. It was really close, but in the end, we couldn't pull it out.

I spent the evening with my mom, and I could feel that she was both proud and excited for me. It was the beginning of an exciting adventure with an opportunity to be and do something great. I wasn't playing in the scheduled games, but I felt that as a young player on the team, there was hope and a lot of room for me to grow and learn. I felt my time would eventually come, and that I would play.

Alabama

After the Florida game, the SEC changed the rule regarding the number of players who could dress. Kyle let me know about the new rule and how it affected me. Non-scholarship players could not dress for home games for the rest of the year. My dad had already planned to come to the next home game against Alabama. I was upset, but at least he would get a chance to see me practice with the team. "It's only year one," I told myself. I could be patient. I knew I would be playing much more in the future.

My dad made it early on Thursday to watch the final practice of the week. As we practiced inside the stadium, I saw him watching through a fenced off area. I had an awesome practice: catching passes, running around the defense left and right. After practice my dad said, "Great practice. That was really fun to watch." He asked me, "Do you know the defensive lineman Poe?"

I replied, "Yeah, I know who Poe is."

He said, "We were both watching practice, and he asked me, 'Is your son out here?'" My dad told me he'd answered yes, that Poe had then asked which one, and that my dad had told him,

"Richie, the receiver." Poe had then said, "Oh, man, that little guy makes us run all over the field. Whenever he scores or makes a big play, the coaches get on us and make us do extra conditioning. He is a pain, but I have to admit he makes us better." After practice, Dad and I went to the Rib Cage for a great barbecue dinner. We had a good time talking about football, the players on both teams, and tomorrow's big game against Alabama.

My dad and I went to the game, where Ole Miss lost again, though just barely. It was the story of the Ole Miss season. Our young team was competitive against the top players in the SEC, and we were just barely losing. We had the talent, but we needed some time to mature. The games were close; we just couldn't pull out the wins.

Practice

Almost every day in practice we did the "Rebel Drill," a two-on-two drill where an offensive lineman and a running back or a Blackshirt were set in a formation. The opposing defense was set in a lineman and a linebacker formation. The offensive lineman assignment was to block the defensive linesman. The running back or the Blackshirt would have to run full speed to get past the linebacker by either juking the linebacker or running him over. There wasn't a great deal of space for sidestepping the linebacker because only a narrow running lane was available marked by cones. I believe this is when the coaches finally acknowledged that I had some real potential for playing in the SEC.

My assignment was against Tony Fein, our starting middle linebacker, who was six feet three and 250 pounds of solid muscle.

Man, he was huge. As I got into the box, I worked past any fear. The excitement of being on the team and getting my chance to shine pumped up my adrenalin. I wasn't thinking about injuries or anything else; my goal was to get past Tony. The whole team stood around watching in anticipation.

I grabbed the ball and the coach said, "Set . . . go." The offensive linemen blocked the defensive lineman, and I ran by both of them. Tony Fein was standing right there in the hole, waiting for me. I ran as hard as I could, drawing on all my power from my four-hundred-pound squat, and put my helmet square into his chest. He fell backward like a tree. I couldn't believe it, I ran him over. I don't know if he also was tipped by the offensive lineman, but I'll stand by my torpedoing of him.

After it happened everybody went crazy, jumping, yelling, and running around. The defensive coordinator ran over to me and put his arm around my shoulder pads, telling me, "You're making a name for yourself, kid. Keep doing what you're doing, you are being noticed. We like your attitude and work ethic." My work ethic was becoming a recurring theme among coaches and players.

The next day before practice, Coach Orgeron was yelling, "Where's the little guy who's going to tear up our defense today?" He was smiling and trying to get everyone wound up. I was standing right behind him, and he looked back, and he said, "Oh, there he is!" and he started laughing. That was when I knew that I really was making an impression.

At the end of practice, the starting offense went against the starting defense. The practice squad stood behind the coaches watching the starters. Coach Orgeron looked back at me and said in front of everyone, "Keep doing what you're doing, Richie, just keep doing what you're doing."

The players on the defensive practice squad started saying, "Keep ballin', Richie." After practice, I was walking off the field with the cornerbacks, including Dustin Mouzon. Dustin said to the corners, "Dang, Richie's a good player. I know he's small, but he's gonna be a stud." I fed on the encouraging words. I would usually say very little, intently listening instead. I used their words as building blocks to boost my confidence and success.

As the season progressed, I wasn't able to dress for home games because of the new eligibility rule. At practice, I still wore the best opposing player's number each week. I never gave up or became discouraged with myself or the situation. I just continued to work hard, keep the faith, and help the defense get ready for the next week's game.

Practice was tough, but then, it was supposed to be. In the SEC, it was supposed be a grind every week. I'd always been a firm believer in getting what you give, I knew if I kept contributing to the team, eventually the team would give back to me.

In my first year at Ole Miss, nothing got me down. Every day I was excited to go to school and participate at practice. I was beginning to experience the university life at Ole Miss. You know, meeting new friends, learning about the best places to eat, that kind of stuff.

After our preparation for the Auburn game, I attended a party hosted by a Blackshirt teammate who also wasn't traveling. I had fun hanging out at the party, and as I was leaving, I heard a female voice say, "Hey! Hey, cutie!" I looked over and there was a very beautiful girl sitting in the back of a jeep. I looked back and said, "Are you talking to me?" She said, "Yeah! Yeah, come in the car, we're going to another party!" I saw another guy and girl in the front seat of the car. I went down the mental checklist: they look harmless, we're in a safe town, and, yep, they seem okay. The majority of Oxford's residents were college kids from Ole Miss.

Getting in a car with complete strangers is a no-no in my hometown of West Palm Beach, Florida. Ever watch Cops? Things are always hopping in West Palm, but I felt really comfortable in Oxford. I was a little shocked, though, when it came to the aggressiveness of southern belles. They were beautiful, and they are also aggressive when it came to men. If they saw someone they liked, there were not shy about making it known. I was pretty flattered.

Getting in the car, I asked the girl in the back seat her name. She said sweetly—you know, in a southern way—"Rivers Fischer." I laughed to myself, thinking: Really, Rivers Fisher, what kind of name is that? I'd never met a girl named "Rivers," and her last name was Fischer. This is when it hit me: I really am in Mississippi.

We really hit it off well. Rivers and I continued to talk and hang out. My friends on the team started hanging out with all of her friends, and we formed our own small group. Every Thursday and Friday night, we would all go out together, and, since I wasn't traveling, we'd watch the games on Saturday.

A few weeks later, I met her mom and dad at the Grove. They were huge Ole Miss fans who always held an extravagant tailgate party before the game. I remember the LSU game in particular. We hung out, laughed, partied all day. I talked football with her dad as we watched the game on a big flat screen. I think it may have been more fun in the Grove, hanging with the fans, than actually being in the stadium. In our discussion, I found out that her dad had also played receiver for Ole Miss, and get this: he was only a little taller than me. We had a lot in common.

As much as I enjoyed being in the Grove, it was really tough for me not to dress and to watch the game on TV as opposed to from the sidelines. I knew I was part of the team and helped get the team ready for each week's game. I also knew my time would come. People in the Grove would ask, "If you're on the team, why aren't you in the stadium?" At first, it bothered me. I'd try to explain, but people really had trouble understanding. I tried to explain the NCAA rules, the scholarship system, and the function of a practice squad. After a while, I was okay answering questions and being met with blank stares. The fans were cool. They just wanted to enjoy the game and experience the Grove. I got it.

Overall, the season didn't go well for us in the win-loss column. But Coach "O" was a master of recognizing and developing talent. For example, Jevan Snead, the outstanding quarterback who transferred from Texas, was on the practice squad. Jeven was going to be next year's starter and the future franchise QB at Ole Miss. He was an excellent player and a top-five QB recruit coming out of high school. Rebel Nation was excited to have him poised to hold the reins.

At the end of the season, Coach O. was fired. We were shocked. It felt like a punch to the gut. I thought it was unfair—they hadn't even given him a chance to develop his vision. He'd brought in all of these studs: Michael Oher, Mike Wallace, Dexter McCluster, Greg Hardy, Jamarca Sanford, Kendrick Lewis, John Jerry, Marshay Green, Cassius Vaughn, among eight others and a new franchise quarterback. But he wasn't given the chance to fully cultivate his players. Heading into Coach Orgeron's fourth year, all his initial recruits would have been juniors and seniors.

Unfortunately, my friend Kyle, along with the rest of the position coaches, was also released. Kyle—my friend, my biggest supporter. The one who had secured my walk-on tryout. I'd built a solid reputation with my coaches, and now they were gone. It was a sad day.

Back to square one. I prepared myself to make a good impression and reestablish my reputation with the new coaching staff. It wasn't the first time I'd had to do this, but I was really bummed. Through my physical play, I created a solid foundation with the coaching staff. They overlooked my physical size and saw my heart, drive, competitiveness, and dedication to the team. I felt good about one thing, Coach O. thought I was a legit SEC football player. It was going to be years before I had that feeling again.

Two weeks after the season ended, we found out that Houston Nutt was our new head coach. He had recently resigned from the University of Arkansas and was now here at Ole Miss. At the first team meeting he called, he told us he was excited, that we were going to play in big bowl games and ultimately win a national championship. He explained that he wanted us to concentrate on our school work and working out, and that in early spring, he would announce the coaching staff.

I did everything Coach Nutt requested. I focused on school and working out; I had awesome grades at the end of the semester; and I committed to major in criminal justice and minor in business. I was really intrigued with the Secret Service, FBI, and undercover police work. I was excited about my major and kept my business minor on the back burner just in case law enforcement was not for me.

At the end of the semester, I was ready to go home for Christmas break. It was good being home with my family. I enjoyed my time away from school, and even from football. I hung out with my friends and felt like my old self. I also began the mental and physical preparation for the spring. I did some light workouts and played tennis to keep my endurance and strength up. I needed to be prepared to train with the best athletes in the world and prove to the new coaches that I was worthy of being on the team.

CHAPTER 7

The New Regime

THE CHRISTMAS BREAK WAS THE FIRST TIME that I had a chance to unwind, see friends, and do a little—or in some cases a lot of—celebrating. However, I anticipated the end of break when I would return to Oxford. I couldn't wait to begin training for the upcoming season and prove my worth to the new coaching staff. I was a little out of shape but felt I could get it back quickly.

When I got back to Ole Miss, Coach Nutt called a team meeting so the players could meet his new coaching staff. He'd been busy over the break recruiting and hiring, and now it was time to establish the Houston Nutt era. The meeting was held in the IPF. Coach Nutt introduced the coaches, trainers, equipment guys, and strength coaches to the team. Each coach was given an opportunity to speak with us. I listened intently to each coach and "drank the Kool-Aid" of optimism.

After the introductions, the players and coaches started mingling. I was eyeing my new position coach and waiting for the chance to speak with him. At an opportune moment, I went up and introduced myself to Coach Ron Dickerson. I think he was a little taken aback to learn I was one of the receivers on the team. I really couldn't blame him; I was off the radar and knew he hadn't heard of me. Standing five feet seven, I wasn't the prototype SEC receiver the coach probably had in mind. Here we went again! This was all-too-familiar territory and something that I battled my whole football career.

As I mingled, I had the feeling that I was a little out of place. My teammates were on their best behavior trying to make a good first impression on the new staff. Some players tried extra hard. I stayed true to my beliefs and continued with the introductions.

Coach Nutt had hired new strength coaches, and it was immediately evident that their philosophy and agenda were very different than those of the previous staff. Under Coach O., strength and conditioning was a priority for all players. The new strength and conditioning coaches were focused only on scholarship players. An immediate class system was born in the weight room. Scholarship players were first class and the rest of us, the Blackshirt non-scholarship players were a second-class afterthought. This was confirmed at each session in the weight room. Regardless of the negative vibe, I continued to be motivated and believe in my talents, even if no one else did.

The next day we began the spring semester. I attended classes and strength and conditioning. From the beginning, you could pick up on the disdain for Blackshirts. It didn't take a rocket scientist to figure out where Coach Decker, the new head strength and conditioning coach, was headed. Instead of embracing open competition and support as the previous strength coaches had done, Coach Decker confirmed his prioritization of scholarship players on a daily basis.

One of Coach Decker's first drills had everyone standing on the lines five yards apart. The scholarship players were specifically placed in the front of the lines and Blackshirts were in the back. I understood favoring their "assets," but many of the scholarship players would have never made it to the front of the line last year because they didn't work hard enough to earn it. Working hard and earning your place in line was replaced with scholarship entitlement, and that didn't sit well with me. I took the new philosophy as an insult and was determined to prove them wrong.

The coaches helped scholarship players with nutrition, giving them meal plans and extra supplements. Scholarship players received sufficient supplements and shakes as needed to gain weight and/or muscle or to maintain body mass. There was only a small allotment for the Blackshirts to share. Coach Decker helmed this unequal distribution.

I would investigate and ask many questions, knowing the importance of nutrition and fitness. Since I wasn't getting support from the coach, I researched nutrition on my own. My best friend from Jacksonville University, Dean Mcnash, was instrumental in teaching me about nutrition. I realized nutrition was a key to better performance and to making this team.

Strength and conditioning continued on the regular schedule. We began our off-season strength and conditioning regimen with an intense warm-up, then learning new moves and proceeding to "test." The "test" happened in the IPF and was not very difficult. The test consisted of the broad jump, high jump, quad strength, hamstring strength, balance, and upper body strength. They used unconventional exercises to test our strength, and they recorded the results using a number system. I'd never seen this method before and was interested to learn how it worked, mostly because we never stepped foot in the weight room.

At the end of the test, we had an unexpected conditioning drill on which I didn't do very well. For me, and what I had shown last year, I messed up big time. My performance on that day didn't create a solid first impression. I wasn't sure how closely the coaches were watching because there were a lot of us running, but it definitely was not one of my best showings.

During the spring, we worked out four days a week, and on Wednesdays we would spend an hour and a half stretching and working on flexibility. We didn't do any conditioning, which was odd to me. I was still learning my body at the time, but I had been down this road before and I did not want to bulk up as I'd done at JU. I wanted to stay lean and get faster. The coach's goal was to get us stronger, but my body was just bulking up. Regardless, I trusted the coaches. I felt I was a little overweight at the time, but I was definitely much stronger than I'd ever been. I hoped the weight and strength translated to better performance.

I enjoyed spending time with Rivers. Our relationship grew as we spent time together, going to the movies, to the "square," to dinner, or just hanging out. The "square" in downtown Oxford is surrounded by bars, clubs, shops, and restaurants. Right in the middle of the square was the courthouse, a beautiful, ornate southern-style building. The "square" was a really fun place to go.

As the spring off-season went on, I continued to work very hard on academics and also in the weight room. I spent many hours alone in the receivers' meeting room watching film of the previous season. I wanted to learn as much as possible and also wanted the coaches to know I was dedicated. I felt that being seen around the facility was important, whether I was watching film or studying the playbook. I was engaged, learning, and working to get better. I would talk with the coaches and ask questions, and I really enjoyed watching film.

I studied Reggie Wayne and Santana Moss, two prolific Hurricane wide receivers who played at the University of Miami. They were both undersized and went on to have stellar NFL careers. The college game film was invaluable, but I also learned from watching practice tape. I studied how they practiced over and over again. I had a lot to learn.

One of the things I struggled with was "getting off the jam." At times, I felt like I did it really well and other times, very poorly. The "jam" is when the receiver lines up on the line of scrimmage and either the defensive back (DB) or the man covering you is in your face in press coverage. "Getting off the jam" is when the receiver has the ability to trick or fake the DB into going the opposite direction or using sheer power to muscle your way past the defense. I reached out to the new receiver coach for advice.

Coach Dickerson (Coach D) was pretty cool. I went to his office and asked him if he could give me pointers on getting off the jam. He said, "It's all mental." Simple advice, but it always stuck with me. Each time I got to the line of scrimmage, I thought about that. It made a lot of sense to me. Knowing the players tendencies in front of you was paramount in getting around them. Athleticism is extremely important, but playing smart on the line is even more important.

As the off-season progressed, we were closing in on the beginning of spring practice. Part of the off-season drills would include a one-on-one session with the defensive backs each week. The coaches' offices were located on the perimeter of the indoor practice fields, so they had a birds-eye view of our "unofficial practice." It was a chance for players to make a good impression on the coaches. I felt good about my 75 percent production rate in the "jam" drill. Seventy-five percent equates winning three out of four times on the one-on-ones. I was constantly trying to disrupt the defense, and I felt some of the players weren't happy about my actions. It didn't bother me because I was being aggressive and wanted to make the most of my opportunity.

We also began having receiver position meetings in Coach Dickerson's office. In the meeting, Coach D would go over basic plays and talk football. Attendance at these meetings wasn't mandatory, but I made it a point to be there daily. Over the previous year, the receiver group had developed some chemistry and camaraderie. Our position group was impressive and was made up of top-tier scholarship players, including Shay Hodge, Mike Wallace, Dexter McCluster, scholarship players who were less known, myself, and a few other walk-ons.

The receiver group was culturally and ethnically diverse. We came from different parts of the country, some of us from large urban cities and some from small southern towns. As we got to know each other, we became friends and grew as a unit. Most of the other position groups would watch us and thought we were a little crazy. We were comfortable as a group and began exploiting our little idiosyncrasies. We had nicknames and specialized in "goofing" on each other most the time. Sometimes we could get annoyed, but we always laughed it off at the end of the day.

First Spring Practice

My first spring practice with the new coaching staff was here, and I was getting my locker ready. I secured my clear plastic visor over my face mask and made sure I had all my gear fitted and in order. I wanted everything perfect so I could gain any and every performance advantage in practice.

Everyone started with a clean slate. The new coaching staff was seeing all the players live for the first time. The scholarship players were assumed above non-scholarship players, but on the first day, the depth chart flattened. I believed the new coaching staff wanted to give everyone a fair chance and promote competition for the betterment of the team.

I will never forget the first day of spring practice; it was extremely hot. On the practice field prior to practice, the first thing we would do as an offensive group was a drill called "pat and go." The receiver would run a very slow "go" or "fade" route, and the quarterbacks would lob it over your head. The goal was to stay to the inside of the ball and catch it over your outside shoulder. It wasn't the easiest catch in the world but at slow speed, it wasn't the hardest either.

I went and dropped the first one with all the coaches around me. Are you kidding me? Not one dropped pass in a high school football game or any scrimmage for that matter. I don't know what was going on in my head, but it happened. Maybe I was nervous about the new coaches or my eligibility to play, but this was definitely not one of my better first impressions. The coaches yelled at me and a few other players who dropped the ball, and then practice went on. Our practices were open, so there were usually a number of fans watching.

The first three practices went very well except for that drop. During the first practice, I didn't get much playing time, but I made the most of my opportunities. I did well in the individual receiver drills, catching my coach's attention. He gave me some additional reps in practice and a chance for more the following day. On day two, I did well in the individual receiver drills and the one-on-ones against the defensive backs. Coach D began giving me more play time in the seven-on-seven as well as team drills. I was exchanging reps with Dexter McCluster. I was lighting it up, making catch after catch and big play after big play. I went four for four that day on the one-on-ones, and the new coaches were starting to take notice.

After my first three days of practice, my reps were consistently up there with those of the starters and second-stringers. I was really sore! I began to regret not doing my own conditioning during the spring. For me to compete at the highest level, I needed to be in better condition. I was competing with genetically gifted athletes. Some players who did not participate in spring conditioning strictly relied on their natural ability to get by. I had to extract every ounce of talent, technique, physical strength, and stamina to even stay close to their natural athleticism.

Articles began springing up about me on the web. They were written by top blog owners who focused on Ole Miss, and other bloggers who concentrated on the SEC and college football. I wasn't very tech savvy at the time, so my dad would alert me when new articles were posted. I was very intrigued by the madness of the SEC blogs—the team loyalties were intense.

I would Google my name and find all kinds of funny names and comments. To summarize the general consensus: he is a walk-on, he's small, but he's a playmaker. Some of the articles were written by boosters and alumni, who made predictions and talked about me being someone who could contribute in the fall.

On day four, we put on the pads, and I was able to show my toughness early. The day was also special because it was the first time Coach Nutt recognized my play and gave me some words of encouragement during the seven-on-seven drill. A seven-on-seven matches seven offensive players against seven defensive with no linemen and passing only. I caught a touchdown on the very first play against the starters. Coach Nutt said, "Keep doing what you're doing, Richie." He and the other coaches were smiling. I always was curious why they were smiling and laughing. I don't think the coaches disrespected me, but there may have been something humorous about a small guy tearing up bigger scholarship recruits.

As the practice went on, the reality of not being in optimal shape began to show in my speed and endurance. I was getting beat up. I felt slow, and instinctively I kept thinking that the prescribed off-season training was not right for me. I knew I wasn't performing to my maximum potential. I had too much muscle packed on my small frame combined with no conditioning or speed training. I performed decently for the remaining six spring practices, but nothing I did was exceptional. I could not get rid of the soreness or fatigued-muscle state.

The very last practice was a scrimmage called the spring game. The coaches split the roster into two teams. One consisted of first-string starters and the other of backups. I'm not sure why the coaches used this configuration. Whenever I watched spring games on TV, they usually split up the teams with more parity. I thought this created better competition and more enjoyment for the fans.

I was on the backup team and started in the four wide receiver set. I had three catches during the game and I believed my first game was a solid performance. The game was televised, and I recorded it to view later that day.

After the game, I felt relieved. Although my performance

during spring practices was not perfect or outstanding, I thought I had built a good foundation to qualify for camp. At least I hoped I had. I didn't want to go down that familiar bumpy road of uncertainty and clawing to make camp again.

I got home and watched the spring game as a "fan." It was cool watching myself on TV at the college level. The last time I'd seen myself on television had been in high school. The local television stations in West Palm Beach would show high school football highlights every Friday night after the game.

At the spring game, the announcers and film crew had access to the players. After one of my catches, the announcers talked about my spring practice. As the camera tracked me on the screen, I could see "Contartesi" on the back of my jersey. They discussed my status as a walk-on, the good things I did during the spring, and my chances of making the team. I'm not sure how many times they mentioned "walk-on," but it was getting annoying. They also said, "He's making big plays but is not intimidating from a size standpoint." Really? I added this comment to my growing list of dumb comments and people who doubted me. I had a lot to prove to myself, as well as to the doubters and nonbelievers.

The spring game marked the official end of spring practice. Now, it was time for my infamous waiting game. I was just waiting to find out if I made camp. Jacksonville had a similar process when it came to being invited back to camp. At Ole Miss, you had to prove you were better than the other walk-ons. In essence, you had to earn the right to contribute, or the coaches would continue to try out other walk-ons or junior college players. You had to show you were capable of playing at the SEC level.

For the rest of the semester, we had some strength training, but it was very light. They weren't very strict on it. The focus for the new coaching staff was getting all the athletes through classes with good grades. The team's core GPA was important to Coach Nutt and the new staff. We still had workouts three days a week, but they were not intense. Nothing like what the summer had to bring.

After the semester was completed, I went home for a week to see my family and relax before the summer training and conditioning. I returned to Oxford to work out and condition with the team over the summer. The walk-ons and non-scholarship players were not a top priority; the strength coaches made that known.

We would do speed drills, and the strength coach would say, "All the guys who run a four-point-four forty over here, and everyone else over there in the other line." At the time, I couldn't run a 4.4 forty. I was running 4.5-4.6 40s, so I went to the other line. Ironically, all the scholarship players were in the 4.4 forty line, regardless of the time they ran, and the non-scholarship players were in the other line. I stayed true to myself, wanting to earn my way on the 4.4 forty line. There was an underlying feeling of separation within the team.

I worked out at 7:30 in the morning group. I always felt more productive and would get my best workout in the morning. We worked out hard for two hours a day all week. Toward the end of the summer, we would come back for two a days and seven-on-seven drills. Our schedule was simple and the same every week.

Training schedule from 7:30 a.m. - 9:30 a.m.

Monday:

On the Turf: Speed training

Weight room: Upper body

Conditioning: None

Tuesday:

On the Turf: Plyometric

Weight room: Squats and lower body

Conditioning: 110s (started at eight and worked our way to sixteen)

Wednesday:

On the Turf: Stretching

Weight room: Off

Conditioning: None

Thursday:

On the Turf: Speed training

Weight room: Upper body

Conditioning: 100s, 80s, 60s, 40s

Friday:

On the Turf: Plyometrics

Weight room: Lower body

Conditioning: Stadiums

On Fridays we would do "stadiums." Just explaining stadiums leaves me breathless. These bad boys are a killer. After we completed our Friday workout, we would walk out to the stadium as a group and prepare for the demanding stadiums. We would start at the very bottom bleacher and would run to the top of the stadium and back to the bottom bleacher in 1.30 seconds. Once the 1.30 was over, you would start at the next rep of bleachers. So after a few weeks I figured out a method to the madness. My goal was to sprint to the top like a lunatic and come down at a moderate pace. This would give me a forty-five second rest. Some guys who went up slowly and then down slowly never had time to rest and always died out faster.

During week one of summer practice, we started off with eight full stadium reps, progressing to sixteen. Oh, yes, how could I forget? If you didn't make the sequence in time, the rep didn't count and you had to repeat it. It's was very daunting. A well-known receiver, now in the NFL, had a lot of trouble running stadiums. He was always in great shape and did well in conditioning but just couldn't run stadiums effectively. That first year, he would usually stay an additional thirty minutes to finish the reps. I'm not sure why he struggled so much.

At the end of the summer, I moved out of my old apartment into a new house with two Ole Miss baseball players. My old apartment was great for the first year, but in reality, it was pretty nasty on the inside. I am surprised I didn't have serious health problems because when I left, they uncovered a large mold infestation. I was just happy to be out of there.

My new roommates were baseball players and weren't there for the entire summer. So, I had this really nice three bedroom two-story house all to myself. Our neighborhood was really cool. There were twelve houses in a variety of colors, each with a yard and adjacent to the pool. I met some great people I still communicate with. Rivers stayed in Oxford taking classes while I was practicing with the team. We spent a lot of time together and had a great summer.

Finally, summer was coming to an end, and the cut list was coming out the next day. Had I made camp? It felt like my first week at Ole Miss under Coach Orgeron again. I was nervous, anxious, and sweating. I anticipated the time when I could get in my car and drive to the indoor practice facility to see the camp cut list.

CHAPTER 8

Golden Opportunities

I ARRIVED AT THE PRACTICE FACILITY EARLY. My hands were wringing with sweat as I approached the door with the posted player list. After a quick glance, I could see my name. In my head, I screamed yes! Trying to be nonchalant—you know, cool about it—I just smiled and walked to my locker. It was the last day of summer training. I'd made it.

We were given a week to relax before the official start of camp. I arranged a flight back to West Palm Beach to spend time with my family. It was a tough time for my dad, who had recently left a job during the worst time of the recession. He finished his doctorate and had finally found a new position after six months of searching. My dad relocated to Pennsylvania and was staying in a hotel while trying to sell his house in West Palm Beach. I spoke with him quite often about our similar and unknown paths into the future. I knew he would find a rewarding job; unfortunately, I just didn't get a chance to see him much. We spoke a lot, though, and he knew how much I cared about him.

On the plane ride back to Oxford, I began to put my fall game plan together as well as a strategy to work my way up the depth chart. I created a clear vision with measurable goals and timelines. I landed in Oxford two days early and had time to get settled into my house. I caught up on sleep and I was one hundred prepared to start the season.

The first organized team meeting was a dinner. All players invited to camp and the new coaching staff sat together, prayed, and ate dinner. After dinner, everyone walked to a large auditorium and we officially had our first team meeting.

Coach Nutt briskly walked into the room and began clapping his hands really fast. He said, "Jevan Snead is our starting quarterback." No questions asked. Coach Nutt made it very clear that it was "go" time, the real deal, no games, no joking, no playing. He told us that for us to win a national championship, we had to be serious about our academics and health. It was imperative for us to study hard, receive good grades, sleep, eat, and drink lots of water. Most of all, we must commit ourselves to the team and football.

Coach Nutt took command of the room. He walked in with authority, passion, and energy making everyone a believer. We were going to win a championship. He was earning our respect, not only for his success in Arkansas but also for his positive presence and attitude now at Ole Miss.

I was a little intimidated for my first training camp in the SEC. My camp experience had been at Jacksonville University, a 1 AA School, with a football program that had limited funds. Now, here I am at Ole Miss, I was beginning camp in a multimillion dollar D1 facility. I could feel the pressure of all that was riding on being successful. Our goal was to perform at the highest level and win the conference for ourselves, the school, and the fans.

The veteran players talked about the tough camps under Coach Orgeron in previous years. We heard that Coach Nutt's camps were known for being a little easier. His camp was longer, at three weeks, than Coach O's two-week camps. Regardless, we worked hard. I was a little relieved when I saw the schedule.

Camp Schedule

7:30 a.m.: Breakfast

8:30-9:30 a.m.: Individual position meetings

10-11:30 a.m.: A walkthrough and morning practice to prepare for the afternoon practice

12-1 p.m.: Lunch

1-3 p.m.: Break

3-3:30 p.m.: Get warmed up for practice

3:30-4:30 p.m.: Individual position and special teams meetings

4:30-7 p.m.: Main afternoon practice

7-8 p.m.: Dinner and a short team meeting

8-9 or 9:30 p.m.: Final position meeting

We followed the camp schedule for three weeks. Scrimmages were scheduled for Saturdays. The team would come in for breakfast, meet, scrimmage, and then we were off the rest of the day.

When I saw the first posted depth chart, I wasn't upset, I was just happy to be on it. I was third-string and behind all the freshmen. As a walk-on, I was at the bottom of the depth chart. I understood that the scholarship players were always given the first shot, but I also knew that nothing was going to stop me from reaching my goal of moving up.

By nature, I'm pragmatic and goal oriented. I've learned, through my self-reflection, that it's better for me to aim high and miss than to aim low and achieve something that anyone could accomplish. I shot for the stars. My goal was to be a starter, and I was going to do everything in my power to be a starter. I had no internal obstacles and only external obstacles that I allowed.

Official Camp - Practice Day 1

My goal in camp was to come in, play my butt off, and start over up and coming star Dexter McCluster. The first day started off with a bang. I was making plays, I made limited mistakes, and I was competing with the scholarship starters. On the first set of one-on-one drill reps, I was given a post route and smoked our starting corner, Marshay Green.

I quickly worked my way into the first-string receiver rotation by the end of the first practice. The coaches ran practice based on player performance and momentum. For example, if a player started slow in practice, his reps would diminish throughout the duration of practice. If a player started hot, the player's reps would increase.

I observed during one-on-one drills that receivers who did well against the defensive backs would get more reps in the seven-on-seven drills. When a receiver did well in seven-on-sevens, he would get more reps when the offense played against the defense in "team." If a receiver wasn't having a good day on one-on-ones, he would pretty much sit out of practice. Once I figured this out, my concentration was solely on one-on-ones and my initial step off the line. Performing well early strengthened my confidence and drive for the rest of practice.

My performance was very consistent throughout camp. The problem for me was that the team was stacked with awesome receivers. There were just too many studs on the team—Dexter McCluster, Mike Wallace, Shay Hodge, and a bunch of others. I felt that even though I was tearing it up, nothing was going to move me up the depth chart. So, what was my next move? I had to find a way to make the travel squad. Special teams seemed the logic direction, based on my aggressive play, but the reality was scholarship receivers were going to be playing before me. I debated how to approach the situation, and I decided to speak with the special teams coach. I asked if there was something I could do to make the travel squad.

When I walked into the special team coach's office, I think I caught him off guard. We had never spoken before and I came up and asked, "Can I have five minutes of your time?" He said yes and invited me to have a seat. I sat down and said, "I haven't seen my name on the special teams depth chart—any reason why?" The coach was frank and honest. He replied, "Richie, I like your play in practice but I don't have any film on you. We've been evaluating last year's starters through game film and know our new recruit scholarship players."

His second point was, "Where would I play you?" He said, "I've seen the way you practice. Keep doing what you are doing. I love your heart, but your size is a killer for special teams."

I said, "Use me on kickoff, punt, gunner, punt returner, or kick returner." I thought that the gunner position would have been a perfect fit for me. A gunner is player who lines up wide defensively and tries to be the first player down the field on a punt. The goal is to make a big hit or tackle, or to stop the ball from rolling into the end zone. I felt I had the will, drive, and passion to play the position.

He said, "Right now, I have key players in each position and I like where we are. I'll keep you in mind and have no problem giving you a shot if anything changes." I thanked him for his time and left. He said no, but I still thought the meeting was very positive. I'm in the coach's mind, and more importantly, he knows how much I want to be on special teams.

Almost every day in practice, just after stretching, we would do the Rebel Drill. This was different than the one we'd done with Coach Orgeron. Specifically, an offensive and defensive player would lay on their backs with the crowns of their helmets touching. The offensive player would have possession of the football and wait patiently for the go signal. On go, both players would flip on their stomachs quickly, stand up, then run full speed at each other. The goal for the offensive player was to run over the defensive player, and the defensive player would try to annihilate the offensive player.

It seemed that Coach Nutt would call on me and a linebacker or safety to participate in the Rebel Drill at every practice. Thinking back, it must have been a little comical when I, at 160 pounds, went head-on against a linebacker who was 240 or 250. How about this image: me flipping on my stomach, going full speed, and smashing into these linebackers. It was like hitting a brick wall.

I never won the battle. Nope, not even once. I tried like heck and gave it my best shot. At one memorable practice, Coached Nutt called on me and our best cornerback, Cassius Vaughn. He was bigger, stronger, and older than me. Finally, I get to go against a cornerback! Cassius was a beast. He was in the physically gifted category. After coach Nutt said go, I flipped over to my stomach quickly and ran full speed into Cassius. He picked me up WWF style and slammed me to the ground. Everyone went crazy. I could hear them yelling, "Ooh, ooh, damn, ooh." I jumped right up but I was fuming. Enough is enough! "He is not getting away with this, he's gonna pay," I said in my head.

Coach Nutt ended the Rebel Drill and we started practice.

I was mad and playing with a huge chip on my shoulder. During seven-on-seven drills, Cassius covered me. I ran a post route right over the middle, caught the pass, and as I was going into the end zone, I stiff-armed him then propelled myself into the end zone. As tensions were running high, I didn't just stiff arm him, I shoved the palm of my hand into his facemask and pushed him back as hard as I could. I repaid him with a WWF touchdown and stiff arm to the face. When he stumbled back, he lunged toward me, wanting to fight. I lost my cool, as tensions were at a feverish level. All my frustrations poured out. I didn't realize at the time, but I messed up big time.

Coach Nutt quietly asked me to relax and get back in the huddle. I was out of control, continuing to yell. It appeared that I was yelling at Coach Nutt. The offensive coordinator, Kent Austin, quickly pulled me aside and said, "You need to relax and shut up. You just yelled at Coach Nutt." I quickly came to my senses and realized what had happened. I'd made a huge mistake. It seemed that the coaches had a negative image of me after that play. And then I broke my finger.

After that incident, my reps in practice began to decline steadily. I'm not sure if that was due to the incident or that camp was ending. The veteran receivers were atop the depth chart and my name was near the bottom. As we approached the week before the first game, I was relegated to the practice squad. I felt I'd played well in the spring, worked hard in the summer, and had a good camp. When it came down to it, though, I was a walk-on, not a blue-chip scholarship player. I understood the coaches were going with the proven scholarship players. I didn't like it, but I understood it.

Coach Nutt's staff handled the dress list and team travel differently than Coach O's staff had. Under Coach Nutt, fewer players dressed and traveled. Players not on scholarship or not selected were not dressing. Plain, simple, and to the point. I found this out very quickly.

Memphis

On the Thursday before the first game, they posted the dress list on the locker room door, and I wasn't on it. Our first game was a nonconference home game against Memphis. It being a nonconference game, the coach could dress the maximum number of players, per non SEC rules. Our coaching staff chose redshirt scholarship freshman who couldn't play because of the rule restrictions over me. Some of the players, both blackshirts and scholarship, were surprised that I wasn't dressing and traveling.

Players and friends tried to console me saying, "Man, you had a great camp, you should be dressing." I was really down. I wasn't good company and didn't feel like seeing or talking with anyone. It didn't make any sense to me at all. It felt like deja vu in my football career. Every time I worked hard and developed a good rapport with a coach, the coach would leave and the situation would change. It had happened in Jacksonville and now it was happening here at Ole Miss. Coach O had believed in my abilities, tenacity, and dedication. I'd felt I had a future and a chance to be a leader again, just as I had at Palm Beach Central. Under Coach O, I was dressing for home SEC conference games, like the University of Florida, when I was just a redshirt walk-on.

After seeing the list, I kept to myself and continued to play hard in practice. After practice, I went home and didn't leave for the entire weekend. I was upset and needed time to reflect.

I spent the entire 2008 season on the Ole Miss practice squad. 2008 was one of the best seasons in Ole Miss history. I wanted to be more than a practice-squad player preparing the team for each game. In my first year at Ole Miss, being on the practice squad was a dream come true. In year two, I had higher aspirations, thoughts of becoming a player on the Rebel travel team.

I was miserable, hurt, and bummed out for most of the season. Not being on the dress list or being able to travel never made sense to me, but it also didn't stop me from playing hard or playing well. I made my time on the practice squad count by playing the opposing teams' best players. I continued to take hard hits, which began taking a toll both on my body and mind.

My frustration and disappointment on the field began to permeate my life. It became difficult for me to enjoy simple things such as going to the movies, having dinner, or just relaxing at home. The debilitating physical and mental aspects of football were negatively consuming my life. Rivers and I tried to spend quality time together, but I was unhappy and not a pleasant person to be around. Toward the end of the season, Rivers broke up with me. Looking back, I really couldn't blame her. Even I didn't want to be around me.

Ole Miss was playing well. We won a number of big games, including against Florida Gators in the Swamp. Florida went on to win the National Championship that year. Our team was extremely talented because of Coach O's expert recruiting. Three of the receivers and a number of players Coach O recruited went on to notable NFL careers. Unfortunately for Coach O, not winning in the SEC usually coincides with getting fired.

In week ten of the 2008 season, we were scheduled to play Louisiana-Monroe. There were always a few small schools sprinkled into our schedule to balance out the rest of our ferocious SEC opponents. This additionally provided an opportunity for players to dress. After a long week of practice, I walked in the locker room and I saw my name on the dress and travel list. Finally! Since it was a home game, I got to travel to Tupelo, dress with the team, and hopefully get some "trash time." Trash time is the playing time at the end of a blowout where the backups finish the game.

Traveling felt different this time because I knew I may actually play in the game. As always, I paid close attention in the meetings, listened to the coaches, and prepared myself to be contributor in the game. We left Tupelo and made the trek back to Oxford. Getting off the bus, I felt the excitement brewing in my body. It was real; I was going to play in my first college game. Not including the spring game, scrimmages, or practices, it had been two years since I played in a football game. My last official game had been in my senior year of high school.

I took my time putting on my uniform. I wanted to make sure that everything from my cleats and side towel to the anti-glare eye black was just right. I believe if you look the part and feel the part, you can play the part. During the warm-up prior to the game,

I was in the receiver line getting extra reps. I was ready to rock and roll. After warm-ups, we went back into the locker room to regroup and then come out of the tunnel as a team. I prayed for everyone's safety and thanked the Lord for giving me the heart, tenacity, and gifts to play football at the highest level.

If I was going to play, I knew it probably wouldn't be until the end of the game. I didn't care. I stood directly next to the receivers' coach, Ron Dickerson, just waiting for him to throw me into the game. I'm ready coach! We were dominating on offense with big play after big play. Two minutes left in the half and we were up by 30; I wanted to run on the field. Only the coach wasn't looking in my direction and the half eventually expired. During halftime, the coaches prepped us for the second half and made some halftime adjustments. I was attentive and really wanted to contribute on the field. We were winning as a team, and it wasn't about me.

As we went out for the second half, I sprinted out of the tunnel, taking in the awe of the stadium and the screaming fans. Hotty Toddy! I waited patiently through the third and most of the fourth quarter before I got my chance. We were up by 52 points and 90 percent of the team on the field were backups. At seven minutes left in the game, Coach Dickerson called for me and another receiver to go in the game.

I sprinted into the huddle full speed with my heart pounding out of my chest. The backup quarterback was in and called a run play. I ran full speed to the line of scrimmage and found the man I was assigned to block. I waited for the quarterback to say the cadence. Then I heard "Blue twenty-two, blue twenty-two, go." I ran full speed at the defender, broke down, and made a perfectly clean block. The quarterback called another run play, and this time I made a block that freed the running back, who ran past me into the end zone. I sprinted into the end zone and joined the celebration. The coaches were happy, patting both of us on our helmets saying, "Great job, great job." I was pumped! I'd helped the team score. I played in one other series, which consisted of two additional runs, and a kneel-down to run out the clock. Final score Ole Miss 59 Louisiana-Monroe 0.

This experience made me realize how difficult it would be for me to earn playing time and play with the first team. I wanted more time to play and opportunity to catch passes and refine my receiver skills. There were many great players on the team and I needed to carve my niche. I had to earn the trust of the coaches, overcome the perception of my size, and create a path for a scholarship. The road to playing and earning a scholarship was going to be a long, bumpy road. Playing in my first game was awesome—I just wanted more.

We went on in the next two games to finish strong, beating number-eighteen ranked LSU and obliterating our longtime rival Mississippi State 45-0. After our strong finish, we were invited to the Cotton Bowl in Dallas. This is one of the premier bowl games in January. We were scheduled to face the eighth ranked Texas Tech Red Raiders. At the time, the Raiders were breaking college football records and finished with an 11-1 record. Their only loss was against fifth ranked powerhouse Oklahoma. The Raiders had one of the best quarterback-receiver tandems there was in

Graham Harrell and Michael Crabtree. Being part of the Cotton Bowl was going to be the experience of a lifetime.

At Christmas break, the majority of students went home, but since we were in a January bowl game, the team stayed in Oxford and practiced right up to Christmas Day. We had a relaxed practice schedule, but man, Oxford is a ghost town when school isn't in session. My day consisted of going to practice, and then just relaxing and playing Madden at home. I didn't have a girlfriend, so I stayed pretty much to myself.

I did have a friend who lived in my neighborhood and was one of the few people who stayed in town during the break. I enjoyed hanging out with her because she was down to earth and, being a huge Ole Miss fan, could talk football. During the break, we went to a casino in Tunica, Mississippi, and celebrated my twenty-first birthday. The forty-minute drive to the casino made a fun day trip.

The team practiced until December 23, and then we all went home for Christmas. We were scheduled to arrive in Dallas on December 26, so I had only three days with my family. The Cotton Bowl Committee paid for each player's plane ticket to Dallas, Texas. The nationally televised game was scheduled for January 2. This was the final year the Cotton Bowl would be played in Cotton Bowl Stadium; after this, it would be torn down. Cotton Bowl games are now held in the Dallas Cowboy Stadium.

I was excited to go to Dallas. I had heard that playing in a bowl game was an amazing experience, with team events and activities the highlight of each night. For example, in our first night in Dallas, the entire team went to a famous steak house and ate the biggest and most delectable steaks. The food was amazing all week, from create-your-own-omelet breakfast stations to nightly gourmet dinners.

The next day it was down to business. We had a great practice and the team was pumped. Deion Sanders watched our practice and then gave us an inspirational pep talk. It was the same day that the star receiver on the team decided to tear me up in front of the entire team. We would normally razz each other in good fun, but this time, he took it to the extreme. I was really embarrassed and hurt by his comments. I just sat there and took it. He was one of the best players on the team and I was a nobody. That painful experience just added fuel to the fire for me to be even stronger and more tenacious in the future.

I didn't officially dress for the game, but at least I was able to wear my Ole Miss game jersey and stand on the sidelines. I was part of the team and participating in the Cotton Bowl, and this game was electric. Texas Tech one of the best teams in the country, and we didn't simply beat them—we dominated them! We were on fire. Late in the third quarter, you could feel the momentum swing our way. Texas Tech was getting demoralized, which was very apparent in the fourth quarter.

The final score was 47-34. After the game, I was looking forward to celebrating with the team in the locker room. The locker room was small and the coaches instructed the players who didn't dress to grab their food and go on the buses. No celebrating with the team, then.

I sat on the bus for about two-and-a-half hours while the "players who dressed" were in the locker room, partying, cheering, and having fun. I had a lot of time to think about what I needed to do in the off-season to ensure I would never be in this position again. I wasn't going to be on the outside looking in again!

The next day, I returned home to Palm Beach to spend some additional time with family and friends. I took some well-deserved downtime and recharged my batteries. I really needed it. There was a lot going on in my life, and I needed to pull the plug for a minute. When I got back to Oxford, I committed that I was going to remove all distractions and concentrate solely on football. I was determined to be a starter next year.

CHAPTER 9

The Signature Catch

WHEN I GOT BACK TO OXFORD, after the Christmas break, I started my new journey at Ole Miss. Sitting on that team bus for two-and-a-half hours while "the team" celebrated the Cotton Bowl victory in the lock room really stung. I was determined to never let that happen to me again. It was now time to reinvent myself and my career by creating a new roadmap for success. I'm going to be a starter! Period! No question!

No matter how down I was about my status on the team, I still found a way to dig down and get excited. I thought to myself, "I'm with a coach for two years in a row—this hasn't happened since high school." In one-and-a-half seasons at Jacksonville, I'd experienced two new coaching staffs, new playbooks, and new philosophies. In my first two years at Ole Miss, there had been Coach Orgeron and Coach Nutt—but now Coach Nutt for two years in a row! The consistency was amazing; it made me feel I had a chance.

I made a commitment to focus on my goals, identify what was attainable, and find a way to measure my success. From now on, I would focus on the bright spots: my talents, skills, and maturing person. The coaches knew me, but my reality was still that of a non-scholarship player on the practice squad. I decided that this off-season, I wasn't getting down on myself. I was going to take this opportunity by the horns and control my destiny by scheduling my own extra work to take my game to the next level.

Again, we didn't do any running or conditioning, it was all just working out, so I went back to what I knew best—Strength Shoes (www.EarnaScholarship.com/StrengthShoes). I'd started using them in high school and they made a significant improvement in my coordination, endurance, and vertical leaping ability, and, of course, they increased strength in my legs. My goal was to focus on the prescribed speed and vertical drills on my own and to continue workouts with the team. The schedule would be four days a week with the team, three days a week with the "shoes." I also started asking some of the scholarship players what drills they were doing, so I could incorporate them into my workout.

I was in the 6:30 a.m. workout group, where Brandon Miller, one of the younger strength and conditioning coaches, noted my work ethic and dedication. Brandon would talk with me, use his valuable time to stretch me out, and watch me during drills. I really felt he was there to help and mentor me.

He was always at practice, and he seemed to understand my situation, know my dedication, and see my talent and potential. He believed that I had what it took to play in the SEC. Brandon started working with me at off-times, even on Saturdays. The team weight room workouts occurred Monday, Tuesday, Thursday; Friday and Wednesday, we stretched and did calisthenics. There were no conditioning days scheduled, and I wasn't going to make the same mistake I had the previous off-season. I began my own conditioning and strength shoe regiment on Tuesdays, Thursdays, and Saturdays.

On the first Saturday, I walked into a pitch-black indoor practice facility to work out and, ironically, Brandon was there doing his own conditioning workout. He was setting up "stations" at the time, and I asked him if I could join him. He said, "Sure. Great news!" I helped him set up the remainder of the stations and worked out with him. It was awesome having the opportunity to work out alongside a bona fide strength coach. His workout was extremely hard, but we got through it together. We connected in a way that began a solid relationship.

Brandon was a big inspiration. He believed in me and found ways to help me. We continued to work out together every Saturday. He also began timing and coaching me during my extra workouts on Tuesdays and Thursdays. He was a legit personal trainer for me. This is the kind of friend he became: he would make sure I had extra shakes, like the scholarship players, and he was always finding ways to help me out.

The additional workouts really took a toll on my body. I knew I would have to work twice as hard to compete with the best athletes in the world, given their natural talents. During the fifth week of training, Brandon had a thought. "Why don't you hold field goals?" It never occurred to me that this was something that might be available for me to do. I thought this was a job traditionally reserved for the punters, who were always located with the kickers and snappers.

Early in practice, the entire team participated in warm-ups and special teams practice. As position practice began, the kickers, punters, and long snappers headed either to the indoor practice facility or the stadium to start kicking practice. Brandon planted the seed, and I was nurturing it. My chance to be on special-teams as a starter! Coincidentally, I overheard a conversation from the kickers that the holder, who was a punter, was going to be a senior.

I had good hand-eye coordination, which is perfect for a holder. My athleticism and quarterback skills from high schools would also help with trick plays or other schemes the coaches cooked up. This was my chance to get a guaranteed spot on the travel team. Once, guaranteed to travel with the team, I wouldn't have to scan the weekly travel list. I could focus solely on holding and wide receiver. More importantly, as a traveling player, the receivers coach would know that I was going to be at every game giving me a much better chance to play receiver.

The next day I went to speak with Coach Shibest, the special teams coach. I said, "Coach, I'd like to be the next field goal holder."

His eyes lit up and he said, "Richie, absolutely, great idea! But you know that you're going to have to practice with the kickers during practice, right?"

I said, "Yes, thank you Coach Shibest! I'll practice with the kickers and do everything in my power to be the best field goal holder to play in the SEC."

I thought to myself, "I'll practice with the kickers and somehow find a way to also play receiver. I know I can figure this out!"

I met with Coach D, the receivers coach, and I told him about my idea and conversation with Coach Shibest. Coach D said, "Why don't you go to practice early, work out with the kickers until one-on-one drills, and then work with receivers until the end of practice?" I said "That's an awesome idea!" The current holder was a senior, so I knew I wouldn't be competing for the holder position that year. What a great opportunity! I had a year to practice with the kickers and shadow and learn the skills of being an SEC holder. I immediately spoke with Joshua Shene, a three-year All-SEC kicker, and asked him, "When do you guys meet and practice?"

He said, "We've already started practicing. We meet three afternoons a week in the stadium. Come out and join us, we'd love to have you out there practicing with us." That was pretty cool. I felt I was really becoming part of something."

My first day at practice with the kickers was a good experience. I think some of the kickers kind of knew me or heard about me prior to joining the squad. I felt welcome. I think my reputation for being a good hard-nosed player helped.

I never spoke with Josh before, but I think he knew who I was. He was friendly and the climate was positive around the kickers. On the first day, I started by watching the field goal holder receive the ball, place it on the ground, then spin the laces in preparation for the kick. After a while, I began imitating the process to get a feel for the rhythm and flow of the position. I asked a lot questions to ensure I really understood the nuances of being a holder. If I was going to be the future Ole Miss holder, I had to prove to the kickers I could get the job done in front of one hundred thousand screaming fans.

Things were looking up—I was feeling like my old self again. As I climbed out of my personal slump, my confidence returned. I rekindled my relationship with Rivers. Some time had passed, and I think we were both ready for a new start. She was really a wonderful person and loving companion.

Hell Night

Four weeks before we started spring practice, I received a text from Coach D that said, "Be at the indoor practice facility (IPF) for a team meeting at 7pm." At exactly 7 p.m., Coach Nutt walked in the IPF. A deafening silence swept over the room. He was very serious and meant business. He said, "I'm going to keep this very brief. We are starting 'mat drills' tomorrow morning. Get a good night sleep and be ready to start work at five a.m. We're going to be doing these conditioning drills every Monday, Wednesday, and Friday."

I was thinking, "Thank god we have an indoor practice facility, because it is freezing cold outside, especially at five a.m." After the meeting, we talked to each other, but none of us knew what to expect. There was some hearsay about what other schools were doing but nothing definite.

I was already doing my conditioning regimen with Brandon, so I felt ready. I lay in bed that night and thought about how I was going to dominate the conditioning drills. I wanted to make a positive impression on the coaches and demonstrate that I was prepared.

I tried to sleep, but I woke up every hour on the hour. I was paranoid that I wouldn't hear my alarm. I kept thinking, "If a walk-on misses a major practice like this, I'm history, gone, done!" I got up around 4 a.m., ate an apple and a banana, and then headed over to the indoor practice facility. I took my time and got changed then did a light stretch. I wanted to be mentally prepared. I wanted to be one hundred percent ready.

As players entered the IPF, the coaches instructed us to line up by position groups around the perimeter of the field. The receivers were in the far corner, some laughing and horsing around. I could see that Coach D was not very happy about it. As I waited for the warm-up to begin, I noticed the conditioning coaches and trainers lining up trash cans all around the field. I knew what they were for—and that they weren't for trash, old tape, and water bottles. These bad boys were for players to throw up in.

The practice started at an intense level. The coaches directed the players to stay in groups and we started to warm up by running laps around the field. After about ten minutes, we were instructed to get into lines and the warm-up drills started. The coaches were really animated, screaming and yelling at any player not doing the drills correctly. I was paying attention, listening, and doing my best to perform the warm-ups perfectly. The coaches were on a roll and were barking at everyone. This was intense, no joke.

After the warm-up, they lined us up in the end zone and told us we were going to run ten 100s, eight 80s, six 60s, and four 40s. All of the run sequences were timed, including a short rest. This was definitely going to be a challenge. There were about twenty coaches involved in managing the practice and also responsible for ensuring that all the players were making their times and not missing reps. I worked hard and finished in the front on almost every rep. Thank you, Coach Brandon and my "Strength Shoes." Some of the players had difficulty keeping up, and some were throwing up only after a short period of time.

After we finished the conditioning runs, the coaches set up conditioning stations. We were instructed to stay in our group and complete a two-minute drill at every station with only thirty seconds of rest in between stations. Keep in mind, this was after all the conditioning runs. Man, this was brutal. I heard nothing but coaches screaming and yelling at players, hard breathing, and players throwing up. This was the real deal, and it caught everyone by surprise.

At each conditioning station, I kept fighting, managing to stay at the front of the pack. I was hurting and paying a heavy price.

At one point, I was so exhausted that my emotions threatened to take over. I wanted to cry but kept pushing forward. I know it sounds crazy, but that's how I felt. I could tell by looking at the other receivers that we were all in serious pain. This was the hardest conditioning I'd ever experienced.

Each conditioning session lasted for about an hour and a half. Things were getting a little easier after each session, and as a team, we were definitely in better shape. After our first week, the coaches began running offensive and defensive plays at the end of conditioning. We were transitioning from team conditioning to spending more time on the football Xs and Os. This made a lot of sense to me, because the coaches were preparing us for the start of spring practice. I was a little concerned about overtraining, especially with my regimen using the strength shoes. All of the conditioning caused me to lose a significant amount of weight. I wanted to be bigger and stronger; instead I was growing leaner and faster.

After four weeks of "mat drills," it was finally time to play some football! One of the best decisions I made at Ole Miss was to set my classes on Tuesdays and Thursdays. This schedule allowed me to dedicate Mondays, Wednesdays, and Fridays on football, Tuesdays and Thursdays on school work. Granted, Tuesday and Thursday were long school days, but the schedule was invaluable during the spring.

On Tuesdays and Thursdays, the receivers watched film together. Coach D would dissect practice film and point out the mistakes and as well as positive things we did at the previous day's practice. The receivers meeting started at 7:30 a.m., which was perfect for me. I was able watch film, get my workout in at 8:30, eat breakfast, and then get to my first class by 10 a.m., with classes usually ending around 4 p.m.

On Mondays, Wednesdays, and Fridays, I would get to the indoor practice facility at about 1 pm, drink a large protein shake, eat a protein bar, get dressed for practice, and watch film from 1:45-2:30 by myself. At 2:30, all the receivers would watch film with Coach D and go over plays for the upcoming practice. At 3:30 we would head to the practice field in anticipation for 4 p.m. spring practice. That is: 4 p.m. sharp.

I would always rush to get on the field early and meet with Brandon. He always took the time to stretch me out thoroughly. I had tight hips, so we would work for ten minutes on hip flexibility alone. By the time we were warming up as a team, I was loose and ready to rock and roll!

Dexter McCluster had already proven himself to the coaches. He was going to be a senior and the coaches decided to rest him during the spring. This gave me more reps with the starters and second-string receivers. I felt good. My speed was back, my confidence high. I could read defenses on the fly and was adjusting my routes accordingly. I was unable to do this in the past.

Also, I was getting on the radar with bloggers. After practice there was usually a blog mentioning me making good plays against the starting defense. That was pretty cool. One of the bloggers created a nickname for me, which I started seeing on the Internet: "Whitey McSurehands." (http://www.redcuprebellion.

com/2008/09/samford-preview.html). There were quite a few other names (e.g., Rudy with a Machine Gun), but Whitey McSurehands resonated with me. I thought it was funny.

The defensive backs were having a tough time covering me. I was on a roll, with over 90 percent efficiency on one-on-ones and no drops. I was learning from my past mistakes and using the haunting memory of sitting on the bus while the team celebrated the Cotton Bowl as motivation. I desperately wanted to be a part of the Rebel team. I felt this year was going to give us our best chance of winning a national championship and I refused to let this opportunity slip away from me. I was really enjoying the spring, my schedule, and life in general. Everything seemed to be going my way.

In the spring, I began implementing the new practice schedule developed by Coach D and myself during the off-season. I started holding field goals, for the second-string kicker Brison Rose during the drills for special teams. I'd been practicing with the kickers over the spring and holding was becoming a lot more natural for me. I was beginning to understand the importance of the kicking rhythm and the psyche of the kickers.

During special teams drills, Coach Nutt would call upon Brison to kick and for me to hold. We were getting in sync. After special teams practice, I would go to the stadium with the kickers to practice field goals. I would miss receiver drills in practice—but no worries; I did the receiver drills prior to practice. Ah yes, my class schedule was a stroke of genius! After finishing with the kickers, I would run back to the practice fields in time for one-on-

ones with the receivers. I started to position myself as a leader by helping out the younger kickers and snappers.

After three weeks of jockeying between the receiving and kicking team, it was finally time for the spring game. It was time to show Rebel nation my ability, dedication, and the reason for my being on this team. Same as last year, the Red team would be playing the Blue team.

On the Monday before the spring game, Coach Dickerson walked in the film room and said, "Richie, I hope you're ready. I have you starting on the Blue team." The Blue team is the group with all the starters. I was thrilled! I took this as a signal that I was in the starting receiver rotation. I'd been practicing with the starters all spring, so this was some reassurance that I was in the starting rotation. I knew there was a new recruiting class of scholarship players coming in the fall, but I wasn't too concerned at the time.

I was expecting my dad to arrive on Thursday and stay through Sunday to hang out and watch the spring game. My dad arrived on Thursday and was able to watch my final practice before the game. Seeing him walk on the field gave me an extra step during practice. I was flying around from drill to drill, making plays, showing my leadership skills, and leading by example. At the end of practice, my dad walked out onto the field and talked with Coach Dickerson and me. I'll never forget how Coach Dickerson talked about my improvement and how I'd moved up the depth chart. I was pumped. My dad and I went to dinner afterward and talked a lot about my progress and football in general.

On Friday, we met in the receiver's room to discuss the final depth chart and the game plan. When I walked in the room, Coach Dickerson called me into his office and asked me to shut the door. I thought to myself, "Now, what's the problem?"

He said, "Richie, at the last minute we've decided to put you on the Red team as a starter." The Red team were the backups that I played with last year. When I asked Coach D why, he said, "We don't trust the other receivers and we need a quality receiver to start who can make plays. You'll have more playing time and a better opportunity to show off your skills. Plus, we need you to hold field goals for the red team." I said, "Okay, coach, no problem."

I felt that I'd earned a ton of respect from the coaches and the team. I wasn't concerned which team I played on; I was just happy to be a starter and play. I put on my red jersey, took the field, and acted as the captain of the Red team. It was very exciting getting ready for the game and also knowing I was going to be a starter, a leader and a captain. In the first three quarters of the spring game, I had four catches for sixty yards. During the game, I also had my signature catch against Marshay Green. Marshay, by the way, went on to have an excellent career as a defensive back in both the NFL and Canadian Football League.

So here is the signature play. I ran a go route and beat Marshay. Here's the best part: I had to come back for the ball and jump over him for the catch. It was awesome. Right after I made the catch, I saw Coaches Nutt and Dickerson running down the sidelines. I was excited, but it seemed as though Coach Dickerson was more excited than me. He ran over to me gave me a high five and slapped me on the helmet. It was an outstanding play and it showed that I had what it takes to play in the SEC. The stadium was packed with more than forty thousand people, and I could hear the cheers after the catch. It was my first big play in front of a large crowd. I remember Coach D telling Marshay, "Richie owns you!"

I knew Dexter McCluster was going to be a senior, but I really believed that this was going to be my year. I didn't know what the future would hold, but I did know that they were not going to start me over Dexter. I really believed they would find a way to get me on the field. I ignored the size and weight issues and felt the coaches would create few special packages for me that would capitalize on my great hands and high percentage catches.

Every player was scheduled to have a private meeting with Coach Nutt after the spring game. Each player also had a private meeting scheduled with their position coach. This was an opportunity for the coaches to go over players' spring performance and provide some guidance regarding what needed improvement over the summer. I stood in the hallway in silence, thinking, and waiting to meet with Coach Nutt. I was excited to hear his assessment of my play and anxious to hear his plans for me next season.

He said, "We're really impressed with your improvement. I've noticed that you are becoming a leader, getting better at reading defenses, and getting better at running crisp routes. Keep doing what you're doing, Richie, and we believe that you're going to be a contributor this year." I could feel the chills running down my spine. This time I wasn't worried about getting invited to camp; I was more concerned about my role as a contributor. I thanked Coach Nutt and said, "My goal is to be the absolute best player I can be and help the team win in any way possible." I walked out of the meeting more excited than I have ever been in my entire life. I had heard it from the head coach himself: I was going to contribute this year. Wow!

The spring semester was almost over. There were only three weeks of workouts, final exams, and then summer break. After my meeting with Coach Nutt, I saw my name listed on the scholarship player workout list. I was no longer working out with the walk-ons and the practice squad. I finished the semester working out with the scholarship players. Even though the final workouts were laid back, I was finally able to compete with the best players on the team.

I went home for only two weeks to visit family and friends before returning for summer conditioning. I came back early and began my "Strength Shoe" regimen to stay in shape and increase my running speed. The summer workouts were basically the same as those from the year before, except I was now working out with the scholarship athletes. It was great because I was able to compete every day. Besides weight-lifting, the skill position players would meet at 5:30 p.m. on Mondays, Tuesdays, and Thursdays for seven-on-seven drills. All of the coaches would surreptitiously watch through the windows. This was my favorite part of the day. I would go out there, run around, and have a blast catching passes. It was serious competition but really fun!

Over the summer, Josh and I continued developing our friendship. We both happened to be looking for a place to live. One day after our workouts, we were hanging out at the pool and I asked him if he wanted to be roommates. He said, "Yes, let's start looking for a place." Over the next few days, we drove around looking at different places. Eventually, we looked at a house very near the school, and we knew it was perfect. We got the place and moved in.

It felt that things were once more starting to align. I went home for the final week of the summer to see my family and friends. I played tennis with my mom and had some time to unwind and relax. As I anticipated my return to Ole Miss, I prepared myself mentally for the upcoming season, the competition with the veteran receivers, and the competition with the rookie class of scholarship players.

This was my time.

CHAPTER 10

The Big Game

ON THE RETURN FLIGHT TO OXFORD, I reflected on my third season with the Rebels. I had a productive off-season and was both excited and prepared to get back into the flow of football and college life. As a veteran, I understood the "process and politics" of college football, so I could gauge my expectations accordingly.

I found the core classes of my criminal justice major interesting and engaging, never boring. I felt very lucky to have an interesting major, not to mention the ability to play SEC football. I developed a time-management plan to incorporate my classes, football, social life, and time with Rivers. The plan provided an effective and efficient method of maximizing my time to do well in class and on the field. With things organized, I was ready for the year.

My new roommate, Josh, picked me up from the Memphis Airport and drove us to our place in Oxford. The beautiful house we had rented in a desirable Oxford neighborhood was perfect! A two-bedroom, two-bath house that included a large family room, kitchen, and, as a bonus, a fenced-in yard. We had hit the jackpot. What more could two college kids ask for? To top it off, we were both "neat freaks," so the place was always in pristine condition. Awesome!

Just like the year before, the team had a "Camp Kick-Off" dinner. The players, coaches, trainers, and equipment staff all attended. When I walked into the room, I noticed a ton of new faces. I knew very little about the new recruits because I didn't research game stats or the rankings of rivals. To me, it didn't matter who was being recruited. I would stay the course and continue working hard at perfecting my game.

There were more than thirty new, unfamiliar faces at the dinner. As we sat down for dinner, I politely introduced myself to some of the new recruits. One had a large Dallas star shaved on the side of his head. I asked him his name and position. He replied, "Jesse Grandy and I play slot receiver." I thought, "He's the new recruit everyone is raving about. Dexter McCluster's successor." It was important for me to get to know my new teammates. I wanted to help provide leadership as an upperclassman and make them feel welcome.

After dinner, the coaches scheduled a team meeting. As we walked to the meeting, I noticed a player who was my size, maybe even a little shorter. I introduced myself and asked him his name. He replied, "Korvic Neat." I remembered the coaches also raving about Korvic Neat. Word was that he was also the "next Dexter McCluster," perhaps even better than him.

I don't know why, but the hype didn't bother me. I recognized that the new recruits were young and fast but, hey, I was no slouch. I may not have had the blazing speed they possessed, but I had game quickness, polished routes, excellent hands, and SEC experience. I knew I wasn't going to be the next Dexter McCluster; I didn't have that type of natural talent. I wanted to be Richie Contartesi. I wanted to maximize my natural skills as a possession receiver with excellent hands, who rarely dropped passes and always found a way to help the team win. I wanted to be like my hero, Wayne Chrebet of the New York Jets.

I approached the year with confidence and energy. I worked hard during spring training to earn the respect of my teammates and coaches. I showcased my dedication and hard work during the spring game. I felt good; I felt I belonged. This was going to be my year and my time to play.

Every year, there's turnover in the ranks. Player turnover means opportunity. For example, Mike Wallace graduated, and other players either transferred out or left because of academic or off-the-field problems. Players leaving wasn't my concern; I concentrated my efforts on being a key contributor.

For the meeting, I sat in the front row, already engaged. Coach Nutt walked into the room, his persona commanded attention as usual. When he spoke, his positive energy permeated the room. I could feel his passion and love for the team and the players. I know he respected and cared about me.

Looking around the room, I knew we had a good team and a real shot at winning the SEC West title. We were an experienced team by now, with a number of returning key players. We celebrated our impressive Cotton Bowl win over Texas Tech, and by the end of the meeting, we were all fired up to start the season. The coaches finished up by discussing the camp schedule, and we ended the meeting with a prayer.

The next morning we started camp. The format was the similar to that of the prior year. I walked into the meeting room at 6:45 a.m. and directed my attention to the depth chart. My name was listed second! My heart began racing as it did when I ran 110s. Jesse Grandy and Korvic Neat were listed below me. Though I felt I had earned it, I was surprised. Having a walk-on player start camp above highly touted scholarship players was a big deal, something that rarely happened. Why? Recruiting. Coaches need to assure new recruits are happy and have aspirations to play as freshmen. Some freshman recruits only pick a given school because they are told they have an opportunity to compete and play right away. I'm not sure what Jessie and Korvic were told during recruitment, but I did know on day one, I was the second-string slot receiver. I was motivated, hungry, and ready!

We didn't wear pads for the first few days of practice. We

focused on technique, catching, and route running. I loved these drills; they were all in my wheelhouse. I looked good at practice. My confidence was building, my performance was soaring. I'd been through camp before, so I also tried to help the new guys through the process. My goal was to do whatever it took help the team win.

After three days of camp, we were ready to put on the pads. I was the first player called out for our first exercise—the Rebel Drill. I kind of had a feeling that was going to happen, but I was ready and knew what to expect. Over the summer, I'd practiced drills to improve my technique, coordination, and speed. I could lie on my back and recover to my feet lighting fast. Speed was my weapon. I could win the Rebel Drill by using my speed out of the gate, and I did! In my first attempt against another junior cornerback, I ran him over. The offensive players were cheering and the defensive players were screaming "Oooohhhhh!" I looked at Coach Dickerson, my receivers coach, and smiled. He smiled back. It was an inspiring moment. I felt the work, sweat, tears, and frustration over the years were beginning to bring some positive results.

Just as things were falling into place, I strained a ligament in my shoulder during one-on-one drills. Man, it was nasty and extremely painful. While running a route, I was tripped up and fell awkwardly. As I landed on the ground, my arm swung behind me and I heard a loud pop. I didn't tell anyone except for Coach D and the trainer what happened. It was between us.

I was hurt but determined to grind my way through practice.

I knew if I didn't practice, I couldn't play in games, and more importantly, I'd lose my spot on the depth chart. The next morning, I remember sitting in Coach Dickerson's office after having a few rounds of treatment. He asked me, "Are you going to play?"

I responded without hesitation, "Yes." At that moment, I think he recognized my toughness.

Practicing was extremely painful. I had difficulty concentrating and performing on the field. I remember being in the huddle and listening to Jeven Sneed call a play, wondering how in the world I was going to physically block the cornerback and nail my assignment. Somehow, some way, I did it, and in fact made it through the practice. At the end of the day, the trainer made a shoulder brace for me to wear. It helped and I was thankful, but man, I was still hurting.

I grinded through and endured the week. On Saturday, we had our first scheduled scrimmage, which was open to the public. I got to the IPF early, got dressed, and was ready to go. As I walked into the meeting room, I caught a glimpse of the starting depth chart and saw I was starting. Yes! In my mind, I jumped for joy, but I kept my cool and at least appeared to take it in stride. Of course I was starting!

Dexter McCluster and Shay Hodge, the starting receivers, sat for this scrimmage. The coaches wanted them to rest and avoid any injuries so early in camp. In the receivers' meeting, we went over the plays for the scrimmage and I began my mental preparation. I really believe my hard work and playing through injuries was noticed.

I ran out of the tunnel and warmed up as though it were an official game day. Man, I excited. It was my first opportunity to start at Ole Miss. The fans and some media began filing in. You could sense the excitement; everyone was ready to get the season started. Let's get it on!

The offense unit jogged onto the field. I felt I owned the place. The first passing play, called "BC," was one of my favorites. My assignment was to wrap around the linebacker, "sit in the hole," and make the catch. That's exactly what I did. Jeven threw me a bullet that I snagged for a first down. I had a few other catches with the starting offense before they changed the rotation to the backups. Some of the freshmen were struggling, not for a lack of talent but for a lack of college-level football experience. The actual game speed and complexity is a lot for a freshman to learn, and in a short period of time. I'd gone through it and now the new freshman were paying their dues.

Everything felt right; I was right on track and my goals were being realized. I was better and faster than last year and more importantly, I was a contributor to Rebel Football. I was excited for camp and ready to start the season.

On Monday, the vibe of the practice was a little different. The scholarship freshman were getting the majority of the reps and I was more of a bystander. I took the reduced reps in stride and wondered if the coach was concerned about my injury or if I was in store for a repeat of last year. My mind raced. Did my reps decrease because I wasn't on scholarship? Was my size an issue? Last year,

I'd gotten down on myself and my play had really suffered. I wasn't going to let that happen to me again. I was determined to keep my chin up and my nose to the grindstone, no matter what came my way. I would not let the lack of a scholarship or my size define me or my resilience to perform.

Jessie and Korvic started to get more and more reps. They were rookies and the coaches wanted to see what they could do. Being green, they understandably had a lot to learn, just as I had in my rookie year. Toward the end of the week, I was sitting in the locker room with an ice pack on my shoulder when Jesse Grandy approached me. He said, "Richie, you'd better get healthy, we've got a big game this weekend." As the regular season approached, I felt I'd gained the respect of the rookie receivers and my teammates, and more importantly, I was still in the starting rotation.

There was a traditional event for fans on the last day of camp called Rebel Day. Ole Miss fans had the opportunity to meet and greet the players, get autographs, and talk Ole Miss football. The energy in the IPF was electric. Everyone, even the press, had high expectations for the season. Yeah, baby, this was going to be our year.

The players sat by position at tables circling the perimeter of the field. The fans walked from table to table talking to us, taking pictures, getting autographs, and being part of the Rebel Nation. I sat adjacent to Dexter and signed at least three hundred items and took more than thirty pictures. Almost everyone knew my name; I had a lot of fans. It was an exhilarating and humbling feeling to be part of Ole Miss!

After the Rebel Day festivities, we had our final scrimmage, which was open to the public. Dexter and Shay played, so I didn't start, but I still got my reps in the starting rotation. I left camp both happy that it was over and proud of my accomplishments. I walked to the car with my head high, ate dinner, and went to bed early in anticipation of the 7:30 a.m. receivers' meeting. It was time to prepare for the season opener against Memphis.

I got there at 7 a.m., and my heart sank to the ground. I glanced at the roster and couldn't believe what I read: my name was off the starting depth chart. I was in shock. After my play in camp, I had expected to be the fifth receiver. My teammates had also expected me to be the fifth receiver. What happened? Was this walk-on deja vu?

I immediately looked for Coach Dickerson. When I found him, he probably could see the shock and disappointment in my face. I asked him, "What happened over night? Why was I moved down the depth chart?"

He said, "The coaches named Jesse the starting kick returner. We believe he can get it done backing up Dexter, so he's not going to redshirt."

As I sat there speechless and numb, Coach D's words resonated in my head. I began to realize the impact of not being in the starting rotation; I was off the grid. I kept thinking how I caught everything in camp and now, my whole season was slipping through my hands. It wasn't fair. I'd worked hard. I had earned it! But you know what? Life isn't fair, and you have to play the hand that you're dealt. I certainly wasn't happy with the decision, but I had to keep going. I wasn't going to quit.

Leaving Coach Dickerson's office, I said, "Coach, you know I'm one of the best possession receivers on the team. I can help us win games, all I need is a chance."

He replied, "I know Richie, but right now this is where we're at. You're going to practice with starters"—this meant I wasn't on the practice squad—"but we're going to give Jesse a chance."

I said, "Okay, coach." It seemed that there was always a reason why I wasn't going to be in the game-day rotation.

I was upset but determined to stay the course and prepare for the games as though I were a starter. I'd been elevated to practicing with the starting receivers and I was finally off the practice squad. I practiced hard and wanted to be fully prepared, ready for any opportunity that could arise.

Practicing with the starters was very different from my experience being on the scout team. In the past, I'd sit in receiver meetings, knowing there was no chance of practicing with the starters. Now, I was given an official SEC game plan, practiced with all the scholarship receivers, and then practiced plays with the starting offense. There was a real possibility that I could play.

Our first game was against Memphis, and because this was a non-SEC conference game, additional players were allowed to dress and travel. On Thursday, I entered the practice facility, praying my name was on the travel list. As I walked toward the locker room, I saw my name on the travel squad door. I took a deep sigh and thanked the Lord for all the gifts he had given me.

Memphis.

I traveled with the team, prepared with the team, and dressed for the game. This was the first time I'd ever dressed and played in a stadium besides our own home stadium. I warmed up with the kickers, and then, once the receiver group came out, I ran over to warm up with them. I still didn't know what to expect, but I was ready. At kickoff, I stood next to Coach Ron Dickerson, waiting for him to call my name. Unfortunately, I waited the entire game and had no playing time. It was difficult watching the other players rotate in and out. I wanted to play and help the team. Fortunately, we won the game, but for me, the experience was bittersweet.

As the team traveled back to Oxford, I listened to the rhythmic cadence of the road and contemplated my future as a Rebel. I wasn't sure how much more disappointment could I take. The wind was out of my sails. Throughout my football career, there'd never been a question about my heart, commitment, or work ethic. Now, I felt doubtful and insecure, which resurrected naggings questions about my size, if I was a good fit on the team, if the coaches valued me, if it purely politics.

I never doubted my love for the game, but on this day, football died in my soul. I was mentally exhausted and did nothing that night. I lay in bed most of Sunday, getting up only for practice. I went through my normal routine with the team, watched film, and then went on to a short walk through. It took everything for me to go through the motions; my heart wasn't in it.

On Monday, my disappointment had taken over. I was hurting and needed to talk to someone before I lost my mind. I called my dad and I told him I ready to quit the team. I paced back and forth in my front yard, dumping pent-up years of frustration as we spoke. I said, "I'm quitting. I'm done. I can't take BS this anymore. What's the use? No matter what I do, I'm never, never, going to play." There was a long pause on the other end of the line.

My dad sat in silence and then simply said, "This is your dream, Richie, and no one can take it from you. You've earned it. Don't let another person's opinion dictate who you are, what you will become, what actions you will take, or have any influence over your future. Don't let anyone prevent you from reaching your dream." I sat in silence. Then he said, "It's at this point in time, when you're at your lowest, rock-bottom, and you're ready to give up that the tide changes and the sun begins to peek through the shadows. Keep the faith Richie and stay patient; your time will come."

I sat in silence and listened. Dad reminded me about my God-given gifts and accomplishments over the last few years. His comforting words began to put some things in my life into perspective. After the call, I lay in bed thinking about myself as a kid playing little league baseball. Baseball hadn't been for me—not enough contact. I'd wanted to quit halfway through the season, but my dad had not let me. He'd said, "If you start something, you have to finish it. It's easy to quit something you don't like, but a winner never gives up and quits. You're a winner."

I decided that no matter what my role was on team, I was going to finish the season and give it my all. Never underestimate the love of your family; they never give up on you and have your back for life!

We started the season ranked eighth in the nation, and after our first win, we jumped to fifth. Ole Miss was electric. In the streets, bars, and restaurants of Oxford, people talked Rebel football. Our fans had us going to the National Championship Game. It was an exciting time. I continued getting the game plans and was still practicing with the starters.

Week two was a nonconference home game against Southeastern Louisiana. I traveled and dressed for the game. Then Coach D put me in for a few plays. Mostly blocking and no passes, but at least I got in. We killed them, 52-6.

Week three, after our win, we were ranked fourth in the nation. Our first real test on the schedule was a Thursday-night ESPN Prime Time game against South Carolina. I received my game plan and practiced all week with the starters. When the travel list was posted, my name wasn't on it. In a way, I wasn't surprised. I was starting to feel that my accomplishments during camp were a distant memory for the coaches. Unfortunately, we lost the game and dropped down to twenty-first in the country. We were all disappointed with the loss.

By week four, I was still practicing with the starters. On Thursday, I was doing routine passing drills with the receivers when I noticed the starting holder limping off the practice field. Though mildly curious, I continued working and didn't think much more about it. About an hour later, right before practice ended, Josh Shene told me the holder had torn his ACL. I asked if he was going to be able to hold, and Josh said, "I hope so," and walked away. It was a serious situation for Josh and the team. Josh and the holder had developed a special bond and chemistry over the last three years. Everyone was really concerned, especially Josh.

On my way home from practice, I received a call from Coach Dickerson. He said, "Richie, you're this week's starting holder. Come back and pack your stuff for the trip to Nashville." I turned my car around and headed back to the facility. As I walked in, I thought about the recent conversation I'd had with my dad. I stayed the course, kept working hard, and was ready when called. Amazing. I felt bad for the kicker and Josh, but I was excited for the opportunity of a lifetime. Starting holder against Vanderbilt. Wow!

During warm-ups, I walked onto the field with the special teams coach and reviewed my responsibilities especially the location of the play clocks. Kicking is an art and requires synchronization and timing. A missed extra point or field goal can be the difference between winning and losing a close game. Despite a few butterflies, I was confident I could get the job done.

I held over one hundred field goals during warm-ups. This was my first SEC start, and I had to be ready. This was center stage, the real deal—no room for errors or indecision. If things went well, I got to play another day. If I messed up, I was done.

The whistle blew and the game started. We received the ball

first and drove the length of the field. On third down, we handed off to the running back and were stopped at the 10-yard line. It was finally time to get this party started. My heart raced and adrenaline pumped. I was looking for Josh but didn't see him anywhere. I looked at the sidelines, and the coaches signaled for the field goal team.

Josh had a tradition of running from the opposite end of our sideline. I thought it was a little strange, but that was Josh's routine. Kickers dance to the beat of their own drum. You never want to disrupt, interrupt, or make eye contact with the kicker. They do what they do, and Josh was one of the best in college football.

As I ran on the field, I could feel my heart beating through my chest. Surrounding me was the noise of a sold-out stadium. As I got into position to hold, the crowd grew louder and louder. I looked at Josh and he gave me the nod to snap the ball. The noise decibel level was deafening; I could barely hear myself scream the cadence. "Blue thirty, blue thirty!"

I opened my hand and signaled the snapper, and he delivered a perfect snap. I maneuvered the ball to the original spot where Josh "stepped off" prior to the kick. Any deviation from the original spot can result in bad timing and a missed kick. I hit the spot perfectly and the ball sailed through the uprights. The crowd went silent. I jumped up, head-butted Josh, exchanged high-fives with the lineman, and then joyfully ran off the field. When I got to the sideline, I sighed in relief. I did it! As a side note, most kickers and holders celebrate with a handshake, but Josh and I decided our celebration was going to be a head-butt. You know me, full contact special teams.

My first SEC game as a starter was official. When I got to the sidelines, I said a prayer and thanked God for giving me the opportunity, skills, and determination to play. The game went as planned; we kicked two more field goals and two additional points to win the game 23-7. As the game progressed, I felt more comfortable in my new role. My heart pounded a little less and my confidence strengthened. On the last extra-point attempt of the game, Josh's kick was blocked. Internal panic! Was it my fault? What did I do? Fortunate for me, it was a missed assignment on the line. Unfortunate for Josh, because his streak of 118 extra-point attempts without a miss was over. On the bus ride back to Oxford, I reflected on the Vanderbilt game, my opportunity to start, and next week's game against the third-ranked Alabama Crimson Tide.

On Monday, the Daily Mississippian was on the news stand with Joshua Shene and myself on the cover of the sports section. The feature picture showed us doing our head-butt celebration after the first field goal. As I looked at the picture, I thought about all the events that culminated to that moment.

The buzz around campus was amping up in anticipation of Nick Saban and third-ranked Alabama coming to Oxford. It was an exciting time for Rebel football. We were ranked twentieth and needed a win to remain in contention for the national title. The players, coaches, and fans were ready to get the week started.

The team's preparation for the Alabama game was intense. Per

Coach Nutt, my focus was practicing and preparing the kickers. In every team meeting, Coach Nutt emphasized how the game could come down to a winning field goal. I felt part of something bigger than myself and empowered to ensure we were prepared for that critical moment in the game. My season was a roller coaster of emotions, from the lowest lows to the highest highs. I kept the course, worked hard, and never gave up. I was starting against Alabama!

During practice, the coaches reminded us of the record crowds that would be attending the game. As I ran out of the tunnel, I could feel the energy of the crowd. The stadium was electric, loud, and hungry for a win. Knowing that I was actually going to get on the field and play was exhilarating. I thought back to Coach Dave, in Pee Wee Football, who said, "Richie, I hope you have the experience of running out of the tunnel with ninety thousand screaming fans." Coach Dave had played a UM and knew the feeling. Well, Coach Dave, now I know the feeling!

Minutes before the game, Josh, the snapper, and I went in the end zone to kick a few final field goals. I could see Nick Saban through the corner of my eye, observing us practice. I think he was looking for any weaknesses, but we nailed it.

From kickoff through the first half, our offense was stymied. We couldn't gain any momentum to sustain a drive. Each time the offense had the ball, I stood close to Coach D hoping for a shot at wide receiver. I knew deep down the odds were slim but anything could happen. As we approached halftime, we never got close to field goal range, and we went into halftime scoreless, 14-0

Alabama.

During the first drive of the third quarter, our offense started out on fire and we made it into field goal range. As I started onto field, my heart pounded as the adrenalin began circulating throughout my body. Here I was, playing in an ESPN primetime nationally televised game in front of an Ole Miss record-setting crowd of sixty-five thousand fans. Who wouldn't be jacked up! As I approached the ball, the stadium grew silent. I knew all eyes were on Josh and me. Sixty-five thousand fans and millions of people watching on television—and dead silence. The silence was more unnerving than the screaming fans from Vanderbilt the week before. As I began my cadence, you could hear a pin drop. I think the fans in the nosebleed section at the opposite end of the stadium could hear me.

The snap was low. I snagged it, positioned the ball perfectly, and Josh nailed it through the uprights. The ref signaled with both arms in the air. Goooood! I sprang off the ground faster than Usain Bolt runs a 100-meter race. Josh and I celebrated with a head -butt and we were back in the game, 14-3. We couldn't mount another drive or score any additional points. It was an upsetting loss, but I felt proud about contributing and stretching my comfort zone.

I played in two more games, against UAB and Arkansas. Then the regular holder returned from his injury and was back in the starting lineup. I continued to practice with the starting wide-receivers and kickers but didn't travel or play another down for the rest of the year. By the end of the year, I wasn't receiving any game plans and my reps in practice were limited. It was clear that the coaches finalized the rotation and wanted to give the starters the maximum number of reps at practice. I wasn't happy with the circumstances but happy that I stayed the course and didn't quit. It was a rewarding year; I thought back to the "tipping-point" conversation I'd had with my dad.

At the end of the regular season, Ole Miss was invited to the Cotton Bowl for the second year in a row. The Rebels would be the first team to play a Cotton Bowl game in the new Dallas Cowboy Stadium. What an awesome experience, practicing with the team inside of this colossal, modern facility. We also had a pep talk by Deion Sanders, who inspired the team. It was one of those bucket-list, once-in-a-lifetime experiences.

For the second year in a row, I didn't dress for the game, but at least I got to participate and enjoy all the perks of Cotton Bowl week. Unfortunately, my goal of dressing and playing fell short. I had a great deal of fun practicing and hanging out with team. I worked to be a positive influence and support my teammates throughout the week. As I stood on the sidelines in my warmup suit, I thought about the year, my accomplishments, and what could've been. I had proven to the coaches that I could handle big games and perform well. I was one step closer to my goals.

After the second Cotton Bowl win, I sat on the bus while the team celebrated in the locker room. Deja-vu. I was familiar with the disappointment and knew what to expect. Dexter was graduating, and I was already contemplating my strategy for next year. Keep positive, keep working hard, never give up! After the game, Rivers and I did some traveling and returned to Oxford. It was time to prepare for the last semester and for spring training.

When I got back to the IPF, there was an award sitting on my desk. I ran over with excitement to check it out. I'd received an SEC Scholar Athlete Award, which recognizes high academic achievement for college athletes. I felt honored. I consciously placed an emphasis on my academic studies, and now I was being recognized and reaping the rewards. I also received an athletic "letter" for my participation as a game-day starter and was invited to the awards ceremony for the team. I walked on the stage with the other starters to receive my letterman jacket and plaque from Coach Nutt. I felt I was getting closer to my dream of being a scholarship starter for the Ole Miss Rebels.

CHAPTER 11

Embracing Leadership

IT WAS MY FINAL OFF-SEASON at Ole Miss and last chance to become a full-time starter and scholarship player in the SEC. I was determined to prove to myself, family, friends, and the world that my dream was achievable. My body of work spanning the last fifteen years would become a testimony of my will, determination, and desire to extract and develop every ounce of football talent within me. I'd been playing football since I was five years old and it was my time to seize the moment. Laser-focused, I harnessed my internal resources to concentrate on football, school, family, and close friends.

I walked into the IPF and received my practice schedule. Once again, I was scheduled with the scholarship receivers. I had kind of expected to be with the starters but was still glad it was official. I didn't realize how much my team play and dedication were being noticed by the coaches. I think it's difficult to make an objective self-assessment when you are so focused on your goals. It was difficult to measure the process, but every small battle won, every catch made, and every hold perfected added up.

I continued to work even harder with my strength coach, Brandon. He created custom-tailored workouts that accentuated my strengths and incorporated my "Strength Shoes" to increase my performance. I was doing everything within my power to succeed. My mom had always said, "Live with no regrets," and that's what I was doing. Speed, speed, and more speed was the name of the game for me at this point. Someone needed to replace Dexter—why not me? I wasn't worried about being "muscle big"; I wanted to succeed with speed. I worked on being the fastest player I could possibly be.

I had been studying nutrition for more than four years and was beginning to see significant results in my body. I developed my own meal plans consisting of fruits and vegetables, low-glycemic carbs, healthy fats, and lean meats. I rarely ate out and consistently maintained my diet. Over the previous few years, I had experimented with variety of foods to determine which foods were friendly to my body and promoted peak performance. My research and commitment to a healthy-eating lifestyle were beginning to pay off.

I was also inching closer to finishing my bachelor's degree in criminal justice. My study habits and classroom engagement produced excellent grades, which aligned with my academic goal of completing all core degree requirements before last semester. This plan would allow me to concentrate on football and then take the easier electives to maintain eligibility. Kyle had given me the excellent advice to do precisely this while setting up my classes during first semester at Ole Miss. I met with my guidance counselor, who verified and confirmed the classes needed to graduate. I only needed seven more. The five I had scheduled for spring semester and then two simple electives in the fall. I was scheduled to graduate in January.

When you start spring practice during your junior year, you're considered a senior on the football field. Markeith Summers and Lionel Breaux were seniors like me. They were on scholarship and had contributed over the past two years. Each played behind the starting receivers over the past few years. Even with Markeith and Lionel penciled in as starters, I could see an opportunity for me to take more of a leadership role.

I walked into Coach Dickerson's meeting room and copied all the receivers' phone numbers into a file called "Receivers" in my cell phone. I was determined to proactively lead and organize all receiver activities. I organized the route running times, the seven-on-seven drills with the offensive and defensive players, and all of our group film studies. The great leaders led by example both on and off the field. To help the team win and to reach my goals, I wanted to become a leader.

Coach Dickerson and I spoke about my role on the team. Coach D said, "Richie, I am excited for you this season. You're going to continue to play multiple roles and be the guy who wears multiple hats." This wasn't something new for me; I embraced the challenge. I knew the play assignments for each receiver position on the field—it came naturally and easily to me. I instructionally knew the plays but still needed the continuous reps and practice to have "flow" in the game. I said to Coach D, "Don't worry, Coach, I'm going to know every position perfectly."

Coach D provided an open work environment, allowing me to internalize our playbook and design my own plays. As Coach D scouted opposing teams, he gave me an opportunity to work one on one with him. We discussed and white-boarded defensive schemes, unique receiver sets, and ways to exploit defensive weaknesses by capitalizing on our strengths. I grew to love this part of the game, the many hours we spent together. I knew that taking on this initiative wouldn't guarantee me starting spot, but it was a productive way for me to help the team.

During the second week of spring practice, I was in the weight room encouraging other players to step it up. I was empowered, leading by example, and giving 100 percent. I would arrive for work-outs early and leave late. I consciously examined how other players on the team interacted. I wanted competition in the weight room, not just players going through the motion to get done. No one on the team was permitted to go through the motions.

The coaches did an excellent job of keeping the timing of difficult drills secret. Rumors were flying about "mat drills," but I never bought into the noise. I knew we were definitely going to do them, regardless of when they started. My goal was to be prepared and get a chance to show the coaches my leadership and commitment. After a few weeks of weight lifting, running routes, Strength Shoe training/conditioning, and film meetings, it was time for "mat drills" to begin. I was excited when Coach Nutt called a team meeting. No, I wasn't crazy. I embraced the opportunity because I was extremely prepared.

The next morning I woke up at 4.30—prepared, ready, . . . and hungry! I said to myself, "My goal today is to be first in every drill, be front, and center, and be the biggest cheerleader for the other players on my team." I wanted to be successful and was committed to helping others become successful as well. I understood what the coaches wanted and how it worked. I would use my knowledge and experience to succeed.

When I arrived at the IPF, I was one of the first ones there. I could see the field was lined with garbage cans as it had been the previous year, and the coaches were in the process of setting up their stations. I could feel butterflies in my stomach as I prepared myself for what lay ahead. I dressed, trotted onto the field, and stood at the receiver station. I was serious and focused. My senior year was dependent on my production today. I was all business.

When practice started, I focused on standing out on every drill. I was first on the line and usually first to finish. Over the years, I had learned how to pace myself, regulate my adrenaline, and maximize my strengths. When you're continuously in the front of the pack and projecting passion and the desire to succeed, your adrenaline kicks in, you inspire others, and you just flat-out feel good.

Being in optimal condition is critical prior to engaging in "mat drills." The coaches quickly picked up on who was in shape and who wasn't. Players at the back of the pack were getting an earful. The coaches didn't have much tolerance for non-performers.

As the drills progressed, I immediately took a leadership role by verbally encouraging my teammates. "Only two left everyone." "We're almost done." "Stand up and breathe." "No bending over." Sure the coaches heard me, but that wasn't my objective. As a senior, I wanted us to make it to a bowl game, and I wanted the opportunity to celebrate in the locker room with my teammates. My goal was to help get the team in shape. After four weeks of mat drills and running routes, I was ready to compete for the starting spot on the team.

With spring practice underway, I felt optimistic about being in the starting rotation. Dexter and Shay were off to the NFL, and now I was competing with Lionel, Markeith, Jessie, and Korvic for a starting spot. When I walked into the meeting room, my name wasn't on the "starter" depth chart. That was reserved for scholarship players. As a consolation, I was listed fourth in a five-player rotation for practice.

My status was better than it had been the year before, but I wanted more. My goal was to be a starter, earn a scholarship, and help the team get to a bowl game. I didn't have the skills of Dexter, but like him, I wanted to have a positive influence on the team. I was willing to do whatever it took.

I opened the "notes" icon on my iPhone and put together an action list for becoming a starter and a scholarship player. The list began with getting to team meetings early and included scheduling a daily time with Coach Dickerson for tips, watching an extra twenty minutes of film daily, taking an ice bath after every practice no matter what, winning 75 percent of the one-on-one drills, not dropping a pass in practice, being a leader on the field, being consistent, helping others around me succeed, and dominating in the Ole Miss Rebel spring game. The list kept growing, and it was the first thing I read every morning.

Consistency was my mantra, which was helpful, because the coaches demanded it. An amazing performance in one practice followed by a subpar performance in another could have a negative impact on the coaches' confidence in you. I had learned during the past three years that the coaches wanted players they could consistently count on.

Every day, I worked my hardest and played to the best of my ability. I left it all on the field. I remembered my dad telling me three things when I'd first started playing Pee Wee football: "Keep your mouth shut, listen to the coach, and have the dirtiest uniform on the team after practice." Simply stated: no excuses, do more listening than talking; willingly accept instruction and criticism from your coach; and be the hardest worker on the field. I took those simple words to every practice, because everything was on the line every day!

My practice schedule stayed the same, because of my unique position as the starting holder and receiver. The year before I had cut my teeth in a few games with Josh as the starting holder, and now this year, more was expected, especially in working with the new kicker Bryson Rose. Coach D made it possible for me to work with the kickers and still get reps with the receivers.

This was Bryson Rose's first year as the starter. My experience as a holder in big games from the year before was going to help Bryson prepare for this season. As leader of the field goal unit, my job was to make sure everyone was prepared, had a timely entrance on the field, and, most importantly, was in sync. Games and seasons depend on a consistent, reliable unit. We were also working in a new long snapper, so leadership was essential for ensuring we operated as a cohesive unit. After fourteen strong and consistent practices, we were prepared for the spring game. It was also my last spring game; I had a lot riding on it.

In the spring game, the teams were split up exactly as they had been in previous years. The starters were on the blue team and the rest of the players were on the red team. Even though I was the fourth receiver on the depth chart, once again, I was on the red team. I was disappointed, but Coach Dickerson said, "You know we want you on the blue team, but we need a leader on the red team." I asked myself whether being a leader and finding a role on special teams was helpful or detrimental to my success. Had I given the coaching staff an excuse not to play me at receiver?

I responded, "You got it coach. I'll do whatever it takes to help the Red team win."

I think Coach D did me a favor by putting me on the red team, because it was a great opportunity for me to show Rebel

Nation my skills. Not much was expected of the re team, so any plays against the blue team were going to stand out. As I dressed, I treated this game as a regular SEC game. In a leadership role, I encouraged the red team that we had a chance to win through our hard work, game planning, and determination. We were the underdogs, so we needed to go out, make a statement, and win the game! Wouldn't that be something?

Our first few drives were strong. The red offense was driving the ball and making plays. Our quarterback threw for a few quick completions, and we were running the ball well. The offense was scoring, but our defense had difficulty holding the blue team's offense. I was pretty animated on the sidelines and was cheering for the defense as if I were a coach. I'm extremely competitive, hating to lose, and I wanted to win because this game would a determining factor for team roles and responsibilities in the fall. I was also in the unique situation of oscillating between the blue and red teams. I wore a red jersey for offense and would join the blue team on offense as the holder for extra points and field goals. I guess it was unusual for the fans to see a red jersey in a sea of blue.

The red-team offense continued to make plays, but collectively we couldn't stop them, and we did eventually lose the game. I was very upset walking into the locker room. I felt that my teammates weren't as upset as me about losing and I didn't want to make it an issue. I knew my play had motivated others, and I had given my all. I'd had some great catches and enjoyed the opportunity to start and play on national TV. I did win!

On Monday, after the spring game, all players had one-on-one meetings with Coach Nutt. The plan for my senior year was to start, play, and be on scholarship. I thought my efforts as a leader, relentless worker, starting holder, and rotation receiver should be taken into consideration for a scholarship opportunity. The odds of securing an SEC scholarship are slim, certainly, because you are competing with the best athletes in the world, and there is a finite number of available scholarships. Being five feet seven, 160 pounds didn't exactly help my chances.

Generally, SEC scholarships are spread among three to five star recruits out of high school and four to five star junior college athletes, nationally ranked. It is practically impossible to receive an SEC scholarship unless you are ranked in one of those categories. I knew of only one player who'd earned an SEC scholarship, his name was Andy Hartman. He'd earned the scholarship before I arrived at Ole Miss, so I wasn't sure how he'd gone about it. Andy and I were both from southern Florida and we became good friends. On a spring break trip to southern Florida, Andy and I spent many hours discussing his path to earning a scholarship. Unsurprisingly, it came down to hard work and finding a way to contribute on the team.

Quick facts: NCAA Bylaw 15.5.6.1 limits FBS football programs to a total number of scholarships to eight-five "counters" annually, including twenty-five scholarships for "initial counters." (http://en.wikipedia.org/wiki/Oversigning). Initially, eighty-five scholarships may appear to be ample, but when you consider the number of nationally and regionally ranked high school and junior college players, the possibility of earning a scholarship as a walk-on is remote. It's even more difficult if you are already on the team. Why give me a scholarship when the coaches can use that scholarship to grab a five-star JuCo player? Scholarships are not a gift; they are earned at the highest level.

When I met with Coach Nutt, he began by saying, "Richie, we couldn't be happier with your play and the leadership you've brought to the team. We're looking for senior players who can help lead the team both on and off the field, and I expect you to be one of these players." He then asked, "What are your grades?"

I replied, "I have over a three-point-five grade point average." He mentioned my SEC Scholar Athlete award the previous year, and from our discussion, it sounded as though he was alluding to the impossible—an SEC scholarship! Of course, there were many hurdles, including pending scholarships and commitments from players over the summer, but there was a glimmer of hope.

I flat-out asked Coach Nutt: "At this point, what do I need to do to earn a scholarship?" The silence was deafening. After about fifteen seconds, Coach Nutt turned his chair and stared straight in my eyes said, "Keep doing exactly what you're doing, and I'm going to see what I can do. You already know where you stand on this team; I don't need to tell you. We trust you and we are going to use you." The meeting was over. I thanked him, we shook hands, and then I left. I was excited and overwhelmed.

When I sat down in my car, I sighed in relief. Four years of emotion came over me, and I let loose. I had hope but felt skeptical. Why didn't he award me a scholarship right there and then? Was it that he didn't have all the information in front of him? Did he need more time to evaluate JuCo players over the summer? I felt that I could control only the things that were in my purview, and I immediately made a decision that whatever transpired over the summer, I was going to give Coach Nutt no choice but to award me a scholarship.

Two weeks later, my junior year of college ended. Summer was here and it was my final opportunity to train before for my last SEC season. Most students went home for the summer, but I stayed in Oxford. At times, it seemed I was the only human being in town. Oxford was a town of about six thousand during the summer. As far as I was concerned, there was no time to relax and go home. I stayed in Oxford and worked out with my strength coach, Brandon, the only other person I knew who was still in Oxford!

My roommate, Josh, graduated and moved back to Oklahoma. I asked the landlord if I could move out of our rented house early. He agreed, and I found a small one-bedroom apartment in Oxford. I didn't want another roommate or any other distractions, because school and football were my mission. Josh and I had gotten along very well because we were both driven and had similar goals. After he left, I didn't want to begin the process of finding a compatible roommate again.

Going into the summer, we had a new strength coach for the wide receivers, and he was awesome. Our personalities clicked immediately. He liked my work ethic and was my biggest advocate. He let Coach D and some of the other coaches know that I was working hard and doing by best. During his work-outs, I pushed receivers around me. I know that was officially his job, but I was there to help him and the team. We worked well together and I think he viewed me as a leaders with an excellent work ethic who could help Ole Miss win games. I was the only non-scholarship player in the group, but I sure didn't act like it. I walked and talked with swag, as though I were the best player on the team. Be the person you aspire to be!

In the latter part of summer, we would condition early in the mornings as a team. One overcast morning toward the end of summer, our starting running back—now a key contributor and running back for an NFL Superbowl team—decided he wasn't going to let me get on people who weren't giving it their all. We were running through the conditioning drills as a team, and everyone was extremely tired. I saw some players slacking and called them out on it. I said, "This is BS, you're a starter. Let's go!" The running back decided he wasn't happy with my encouraging words and said, "Shut up!"

I said, "Bro, don't you want to win games?" He didn't say anything but just glared at me. I was amped up and said, "Everyone on this team matters. I'm a senior, and I want to go out with a bang. I want to play in a national championship game, and I want to cheer and celebrate in the locker room." Apparently, he wasn't happy with my response because he came at me swinging. I dodged his punches and started swinging back to protect myself. Neither of us made any real contact, and eventually the coaches broke it up. He was much bigger than I was but I didn't care. I was fighting for myself and the team, and I wasn't going to be stopped or intimidated by anyone. This was our season—no underclassmen scholarship stud was going to stand in our way.

Later that day, I met with Coach Nutt. I think he could see how much I cared about getting the most out of our team and winning. Coach Nutt was an advocate and I could feel the wheels turning in regard to our scholarship conversation. Again he sat in silence behind his desk and said, "You know what, I need to make some phone calls." Coach Nutt made a phone call to one of the campus administrators and said, "I have a walk-on that I want to put on scholarship. What do we need to do?" I couldn't hear the other end of the call, but I sat silently and strained to listen. At the conclusion of the call, Coach Nutt said, "I need you to walk over to the administrative office and talk with Karen." I jumped up ten feet out of the chair and said, "Absolutely, I will go over right now."

He said, "Okay, shoot me a text and let me know how it goes."

When I arrived at the administrator office, I was greeted by Karen, who said, "Hello Richie, we have a few things we're juggling right now. Hopefully, over the summer, we can put things together for you." I wasn't exactly sure what this meant, but I prayed that what they were trying to do was exactly what I wanted to happen. I was anxious but figured they needed some more time. Over the next few days, I received a few reference phone calls regarding my grades and inquiries about my intentions for next semester. The administrators were gathering the information they needed, but I still didn't know what to expect.

I couldn't have been any more motivated as we wrapped up the summer training. Every Friday, we still did "stadiums," and I continued to dominate the drill. I think some of the players looked at conditioning as just another workout, but I considered it a strategy. I applied the entire body of knowledge for training, conditioning, and dieting to increase and leverage my natural abilities. I dedicated the time to figure out how my body functioned at an optimal level, and now it was paying dividends.

Over the summer, I worked on strength, speed, flexibility, and receiver skills, and I refined myself as a leader. I continued striving to be the best I could be. On the last day of conditioning and summer training, the coaches set up stations, and the receivers were together as a group. These drills were the culmination of what had been done during the summer, and over my career. I was mostly in the front of the line, playing all out, cheering others on, and just flat-out having fun. After the final rep, the strength coach came up to me and shook my hand. He said, "Wow, I just want to let you know that you have been an inspiration. I admire your work ethic and it was a pleasure training you. Good luck this season!" I said "Thank you, Coach. Thanks for everything you've done for me. It was inspiring and pleasure to train with you as well."

I was so amped and ready for the season. It was go time, baby! My time to shine. I stayed in Oxford for the final week, before fall semester, because I didn't want to risk being even a little out of shape. I continued my eating and exercise routine. I was cut, ripped, and ready to get the season started. I waited that week on a call from Coach Nutt or Karen regarding the scholarship, but I'd yet heard nothing back. What did I still need to do? Well, at least one of my goals was accomplished—I was named the starting holder for the season!

CHAPTER 12

Defying the Odds

IN THE FALL OF 2010, I entered my final season at Ole Miss. Having redshirted my first year at Jacksonville University, I was exercising my option to play as a fifth-year senior at Ole Miss. A redshirt athlete is intentionally not on the official "active" team roster for the first year of college eligibility, extending the athlete's eligibility for an additional year, usually to allow for growth, maturity, and development of football skills. It was a great situation, because my core classes were complete, and now I could concentrate solely on football. Shay and Dexter had graduated, and it was my opportunity to shine. In my final year, I was determined to make an impact as a starting scholarship player.

Fall camp was similar to how it had been in previous years at Ole Miss. Our tradition started the day before camp with a team dinner, followed by an inspirational message from Coach Nutt, followed by a position team meeting. I was attentive and wanted to savor every minute of the season. For the next two weeks, my life would revolve around football.

I set my expectations in camp. I knew the routine, the system, and, most importantly, what the coaches wanted to see. I learned how to pace myself and work smarter, not harder. I had done the heavy lifting, and all needed now was opportunity. Many players expressed the difficulty of camp and "mat drills," but I had a different approach. My goal was to play hard, play smart, and take care of my body after practice. My routine involved taking ice baths, drinking plenty of water, and sleeping at least eight to nine hours a night. Following this pattern allowed me to play my hardest and leave everything out on the field every day. I remember sitting in the cold tub for ten minutes, thinking, "Man, that was brutal." But I knew that those precious or torturous minutes would pay large dividends the next day. I wouldn't be sore. I looked to my left and right and realized I was usually the only one in the cold tubs. Call me crazy, but it worked!

We would have receiver meetings after dinner. I did my homework and could answer any question related to routes, positions on the field, or plays posed by the coaches. I enjoyed helping the new recruits and younger players acclimate to the team as well as the SEC. I was playing well, killing it on the one-on-ones, and getting some accolades from the fans. I never lost focus of my three goals: earning a scholarship, becoming a starting receiver in the SEC, and leading the team to a national championship. I built my confidence to the point that I believed I was the best player on the field and deserved to be a starter.

At the start of camp, Jeremiah Masoli, a quarterback transfer from Oregon, arrived in Oxford. At Oregon, Jeremiah had experienced a few issues and now needed a new start. Our quarterback, Jevan Snead, had left Ole Miss a year early for the NFL, and we were presently in need of an established quarterback. When Jeremiah arrived and I had the opportunity to speak with him, I was impressed and understood why Coach Nutt had taken a chance on him. We had Nate Stanley in the wings, ready to start, but Jeremiah was a star with a solid resume that included a Rose Bowl appearance. I had an opportunity to run routes and plays with Jeremiah after practice. He wasn't your prototype SEC quarterback—he was five feet eleven, 220 pounds, but he was an excellent athlete with a cannon for an arm.

Unlike in prior years, I was the starting number-four receiver on the depth chart and second at my "slot" receiver position. As camp progressed, I began to notice the coaches cutting down on my reps. Once I recognized the pattern, I immediately took action. The following morning, I came early to have a one-on-one meeting with Coach D. When I arrived, I went into him office, shut the door, and asked, "Why are my reps getting cut?" He gave a long, drawn-out, complicated explanation and concluded by saying, "You're the starting holder. The kicker is more confident if you're holding and yelling the cadence, and we can't risk you getting hurt!" I was upset. I'd worked so hard at receiver and also at helping the kicking unit mature; now Coach D was telling me

I couldn't be a starting receiver because I was more valuable as a field goal holder. I replied, "Really?"

I had crafted a starting role as the field goal holder to guarantee myself a travel spot and to play receiver. I said to Coach D, "You said this is what I needed to do to help the team and to get me in the receiving game plan."

Coach Dickerson replied, "I understand, Richie, but this is a direct request from Coach Shibest, the head special teams coach." I leaned forward in my chair and put my head inside my hands. I couldn't believe it! I felt betrayed, deflated, and upset.

I looked above my own self-interest, thinking of my team and my commitment to help Ole Miss win a national title. Sure, I was disappointed, but I started looking at the big picture. I lifted my chin, looked Coach Dickerson in the eye, and said, "Okay, coach, you got it. I'll do everything in my power to be the best field goal holder in the SEC. I also want to continue practicing my receiver drills as if I'm a starter."

Coach D replied, "Richie, that's exactly what we want you to do." I stood up, walked out, and began my daily routine. I was committed to doing whatever my team needed, including this. I was resolved to be the solution, not the problem, and to help the team win.

After two weeks of practice, I continued taking advantage of my minimum reps as a receiver. I made every rep count by not missing catches and performing at the highest level. I was excited because the next day was Rebel Day. We got to sign autographs, hang out with the fans, and play our final scrimmage before the start of the season. Over the last few weeks, I had continued following up with Coach Nutt regarding the status of my football scholarship, but there had been no definitive answer.

I had dinner, tried to relax, and went to bed early so I could be my best for Rebel Day. Just before falling asleep, I thought about the importance of tomorrow's scrimmage and how it could be a determining factor in earning a D1 scholarship. If I played "lights-out" tomorrow, I'd give Coach Nutt no choice but to put me on scholarship. It may not have been realistic, but it was my dream and that's the way I felt about it. I recognized, logically, that getting a scholarship was a longshot, but I liked my chances of beating the odds.

I walked into the IPF, bright and early. I was ready for Rebel Day, the biggest day of my life. I took every stride as if I was Jerry Rice preparing for game day. I sat down at the receivers' table and began signing autographs, taking pictures with fans, and focusing on what was to come. My goal was to dominate the scrimmage and walk out of the stadium with a scholarship. After we completed the Rebel Day festivities, I put my uniform on in the locker room and then began the trek into the stadium. Focused and driven, I walked into the stadium on a mission.

I met with Brandon, the strength coach, to get an early stretch. After pre-practice warm-ups, the entire team gathered for our regular warm-ups, which consisted of stretches, calisthenics, and running plays "on air." Running plays "on air" consisted of the offense lining up in formation and basically "going through the motions" of an offensive play. This was our normal routine before every practice. We huddled up on the 15-yard line, sprinted to the 10-yard line, ran the play, and then sprinted into the end zone in sequence. I positioned myself in the first group, leading the pack after each play.

Toward the end of warm-ups, I felt a tap on my shoulder. I turned my head to see Coach Nutt pointing in my direction. He said, "I just want to let you know you're now on scholarship. You've earned it." He smiled, turned, and briskly walked away. Shortly after, he blew the whistle signaling the team to meet in the middle of the field. I was in shock! In spite of the odds, I had done it!

I hadn't been prepared to hear this, the best news of my life; it caught me completely off guard. The feeling in my body was that of pandemonium—excited, joyful pandemonium. I wanted to tell everyone who was there for me that I had done it. I'd finally earned the scholarship of a lifetime. An Ole Miss SEC scholarship! I wanted to call my family and scream at the top of my lungs with the good news. I was overcome with a storm of emotions, not knowing if I should laugh, scream, or cry. My work across the last fifteen years had come to fruition. I had reached my biggest goal, and no one could ever take this moment from me.

I sprinted to the middle of the field with the biggest smile on my face. I'm not sure how I even got there, because I don't think my feet ever touched the ground. I was on Cloud Nine. As the team huddled up, Coach Nutt told us that the scrimmage was live and he wanted us to play hard. He finished with, "Remember we're teammates, so let's play safe and finish camp strong."

What followed was the best scrimmage of my life. I had some big catches, hit all of my assignments, and had perfect holds for Bryson, the field goal kicker. In the past, I had created confidence through my faith, but now my confidence was fueled to an even higher level by my accomplishments. After the scrimmage, I ran back to the locker room to call my parents and Rivers; I couldn't wait to give them the awesome news. Sure, Rivers and I had had some ups and downs, but she was always there for me, as were my mom and dad.

The locker room was crowded, and I wanted some privacy for this special moment. I changed into my street clothes faster than Speedy Gonzales, ran out to my truck, shut the door, and then screamed at the top of my lungs. I put the truck in drive, put on my headphones, and called my dad. I said "Guess what? . . . I'm officially a scholarship athlete at the University of Mississippi— Ole Miss! D1 baby! SEC!" My dad almost jumped through the phone. I could feel his excitement, pride, and love for me. I laughed.

He said, "Oh my god, oh my god, oh my god! You did it, Richie, and I couldn't be more proud of you."

I said, "Thanks, Dad, I couldn't have done it without you. I need to call Mom, but I'll call you back." I then proceeded to call my mom and Rivers, sharing with them the big news. Over the phone, I could hear them jumping with joy. This is what it's all about: sharing your biggest dreams and accomplishments with the ones you love, those who helped you reach the highest heights. I went home that night excited and knowing there was much to do. I still had catches to make, field goals to hold, and a team to help win a national championship. I told myself to take a deep breath and enjoy the moment. That night, I fell asleep with the biggest smile on my face recorded by man!

As a scholarship player, I understood my place and value to the team. After speaking with Coach D, I understood that I wouldn't be in the immediate starting rotation because of my holding duties, but I felt that my receiving talents could eventually be used to win games. Since I was on scholarship, I think Coach Dickerson may have had some additional incentive in giving me a shot. I wasn't as concerned about being on the field for the first play of the game, or if I was considered a starter, because I was going to find a way to help the team win games every week. Game one, against Jacksonville State (JS), was right around the corner, and we were ready. JS, a Division 1-AA school, wasn't expected to beat us. For those playing the home game, 1-AA schools are smaller state or private schools with football programs that have limited funding, so it would be extremely difficult for a 1-AA school to beat an SEC Division-1 school.

Our practice and game schedules were established well before the season started. Traditionally, no practice on Monday. We let our bodies heal and recover while mentally prepping for a week of practice. Tuesday was officially the first day of the practice week. We started practice in full pads and then progressed to heavy contact between the offensive and defensive units. We implemented our core game plan and didn't get off the field until Coach Nutt was satisfied with both the game plan and our execution.

This particular Tuesday was also important because I'd find out if I was in the game plan with the receivers. The receivers who were in the rotation received a game plan with their uniform number on the cover. It contained our core plays, strategies, statistics, and information about the opposing team. It was a thorough strategic and operational document. I read individual and team statistics and reviewed how our stats matched up against those of our opponents. I could also review information such as their names, height, weight, birthdays, photos, and more. Heck, I probably knew their favorite food.

I walked into the meeting room, prior to practice, repeating a mantra in my head. "Please have a packet, please have a packet, please have a packet." My eyes darted to my desk. Yes, there it was: a packet with a big red 84 and Jacksonville State on the cover. Yep, this time I was with the starters and getting reps in the starting rotation. I was on scholarship, in the starting rotation, a special teams holder, and key contributor for the SEC Ole Miss Rebels.

The first week of practice was a breeze compared to the Death Valley days of being a human hitting dummy and running one hundred back-to-back plays on the practice squad. I played hard and consistently. It was a relief knowing I didn't have to worry about making the dress-list every Thursday; that was all in the rear-view mirror. Thursdays now had a very different meaning for me; Thursday was the last day of practice before walk-throughs and travel on Friday. The coaches didn't give any information about who was starting or how much playing time we would get. I kept playing hard and keeping the faith that my time would come.

Traveling with the starters was an honor. The morning of the game represented my favorite aspect of traveling. We'd wake up, have a short Bible study, then eat our pre-game meal. It was a gourmet breakfast including steak, eggs, potatoes, oatmeal, grits, cereal, and fruit—practically anything any way you wanted it. On the morning of the Jacksonville State game, I was so excited and nervous that I could eat only a quarter of the food on my plate. Nobody said a word at breakfast or while we were getting on the bus back to Oxford.

As we approached the campus, I could feel my heart beating faster. We arrived and disembarked from the bus to begin the Walk of Champions. I was pumped, slapping high fives to fans on my left and right. Thousands of cheering fans were excited for the new season to begin. As we approached the end of the Walk of Champions, I focused on the game and what this moment meant to me. It was a rewarding to know I was truly a part of this team, to know that I was going to play, and to know I had an opportunity to help us win.

I fantasized about making the big play and scoring the winning touchdown. I was determined to make an impact. I sat at my locker surveying my surroundings while the music pumped in my ears. I went through my checklist: program, pack of gum, socks, jersey, and pants. The equipment managers did a great job of setting up everything. I finished getting dressed, said a prayer of thanks for this moment, and then prepared for warm-ups with the kickers.

I walked onto the field, took in a panoramic view of the stadium, breathed in deeply, and jogged over to Brandon to stretch. As our strength coach, he had it down to a science; he really knew how to effectively stretch my body. After stretching, I warmed up with the kickers, then the receivers, and then it was game time!

The team ran back into the locker room anxiously, waiting for the signal to run out of the tunnel. It was in the tunnel that the feeling came over me: today was my day. I'd play receiver, hold kicks, and dominate this game. I ran out of the tunnel, spinning and jumping in excitement. The fans screamed at the top of their lungs, and I could feel the bass and volume of sound rumbling through my body.

We started hot from the kickoff. We scored quickly. We'd begun our domination. I ran on the field and successfully held extra points and field goals. I stood next to Coach D and Coach Nutt with my helmet strapped, waiting for the moment when one of them would call my number. Having practiced in the rotation, I was ready and itching to get into the game. I just kept locking eyes with Coach Dickerson, fired up, with my helmet on, hungry to play!

We established a nice lead, but things started to unravel little by little. Jacksonville got on a hot streak and continued to score. Everyone in the stadium was in shock. Who could believe that a small Division 1-AA school could beat an SEC football team at home in their own stadium? With less than a minute to play,

Jacksonville State made one miraculous play after another and took the lead. We had time for a final drive. I was ready to get into our five-receiver set, just as we had practiced in rotation drills. To my dismay, we stayed in a four-receiver set formation and I didn't have the opportunity to get on the field. Masoli threw a few incompletions and the game was over. We lost. I was stunned. I hadn't even gotten on the field as receiver to help the team win. Losing to a 1-AA school was disappointing and demoralizing for the team, the football program, and our fans.

The following week, we had Tulane on our schedule. We worked hard in practice to correct the mistakes we'd made in week one. It was really frustrating for me, because as the leader of the receiver core, I wasn't playing. My main job was holding field goals. You can imagine how difficult it was to maintain a leadership role and the respect of my peers when I wasn't even playing receiver. Difficult as it was, I just stayed the course and continued to be a leader.

Although I was disappointed, because I hadn't played receiver, I remained grateful: I was the starting holder, I was traveling, and I was on scholarship. Pretty awesome. Though I did still have a big goal to accomplish. I wanted to complete a few passes as a receiver in SEC conference games.

As the starting holder, I wasn't running very much in practice. My time was limited with the receivers and I was concerned about losing game speed and any chance of playing. I had to be ready, so I created a routine to maintain my speed. On Monday mornings, I'd run a series of twenty-five-yard sprints, and on Wednesday mornings I would run fifty-yard sprints and either 110s or half-gassers for conditioning. A half-gasser is when you run fifty yards, stop, and then run fifty yards back.

Since I incorporated extra speed training on Monday and Wednesday mornings, I felt that I could maintain my edge. I was now running Monday, Tuesday, Wednesday, and Thursday increasing my reps, sprints, and routes. My biggest fear was losing the speed and fitness I'd worked so hard to attain over the summer. I felt confident that I'd be fast and ready to play when my number was called!

In addition to playing football, I was also preparing for the business career I would embark on after graduating from Ole Miss. I needed to dedicate quality time to find an interesting job and career. One of my classes, focused on applying for jobs, was given at the school's career center. I applied for every job on the board, scheduling about six interviews a week. After a while, I knew that the person who was positive, persistent, and patient was going to get the job. I wanted to have a job when I graduated because I had no plans to move home, especially after living on my own the past few years. I love my parents, but I wanted to make it on my own.

Our season was now almost at the halfway mark, and our record was 3-2. We were practicing hard but the scoreboard didn't reflect the sweat, heart, and soul of our team. The first five games of the season were all nonconference, except for a loss to Vanderbilt. Every week in practice, I stood patiently waiting. Coach Nutt and Coach Dickerson both encouraged me to "sit tight, sit tight, be patient, be patient!" That's what I did. I stayed patient, stayed positive, and stayed persistent.

The following game was against the eighth-ranked Alabama Crimson Tide. The Tide was coming off their first loss of the season and had dropped seven spots in the national rankings. Traveling to Tuscaloosa for the game was thrilling. You could sense the passion these fans had for this game as we pulled up to the stadium and were surrounded by tens of thousands of screaming fans. It was mayhem! This was a pivotal, must-win game if we were to salvage our season.

Warming up in that stadium was insane. The sheer size of the building was overwhelming, and then there were the 102,000 screaming Tide fans—the house was rocking. We struggled offensively in the beginning of the game, going three-and-out on our first three possessions, but our defense kept us in it because we played lights out. We eventually lost the game. I did my job successfully on field goal and point-after attempts but didn't have an opportunity to get on the field as a receiver.

We were next scheduled to play Arkansas, making a very special match-up to Coach Nutt, who had come to Ole Miss from Arkansas. At Tuesday's practice, Coach Shebest, the special teams coach, called me into his office and said, "Richie, I've got something special for you this week."

I said "Really! What do you have for me?"

He said, "We have a fake where you run the ball right up the gut." Then and there, I got butterflies. Oh boy—it was touchdown time! We practiced the play all week, and we were prepared, ready to execute the fake. The fake had to be run off of the left hash because of the way Arkansas lined up against field goals on that hash. We started the game slowly and were trailing 21- 0 halfway through the second quarter. Just as it appeared the game was slipping through our fingers, we drove down the length of the field and brought ourselves into perfect position for the fake field goal we'd been practicing. The coaches decided to run a running play on third down to position the ball on the left hash mark. The ball was handed off to the running back, who cut right and ran across the field. We lost yardage, and also the ball was positioned on the right hash mark. Running the fake was no longer an option. We ran out onto the field for the field goal and took care of business, putting three points on the board. After two lightning delays and a touchdown pass to Markeith Summers, the momentum quickly changed in our favor putting us right back in the game with a score of 31-24.

With less than four minutes left in the game, we had five receivers on the field and we were driving to the end zone. I was standing there ready to go, warmed up, doing high knees—and hungry! Finally, Coach Dickerson looked at me and said, "Richie, go to Z, go to Z, go to Z!" and I bolted into that game, full speed. I didn't have time to get nervous. I was razor-focused and jumped right into the no-huddle offense. In a no-huddle offense all the plays are called at the line of scrimmage. I accidently ran past my assigned location but quickly repositioned myself. I looked at the quarterback and got the signal for my route, a five-yard stop route. This play requires the receiver to run five yards, making the defender think you are running a deep go route, but then you slam on the breaks. The play started, I ran the stop route, and Jeremiah began scrambling to my side of the field. The corner came down to cover me and I flipped behind him and I started to run a go route. Jeremiah drilled a bullet to my back shoulder. I spun, caught it, and tapped two feet before falling out of bounds. It was a textbook back-shoulder sideline pass. He couldn't have thrown a better ball for me to catch. I finally got my first official SEC catch!

I was so focused I couldn't hear the eighty thousand fans in the stands. Oddly enough though, I heard some of the players on the Arkansas sideline saying, "Whoa! That guy is tiny . . . holy smokes!" I just ignored them, jumped up, and got right back on the line, ready for the next play. During the next few plays, I ran my routes and got open, but Jeremiah kept scrambling to the opposite sideline. On the last play of the game, I was running my route across the field trying to get Jeremiah's attention, but the ball was thrown deep for an incomplete. We lost the game. I had mixed emotions as I walked back to the locker room. I was upset that we lost the game, but I also had this sense of accomplishment for making my first SEC catch in front of a crowd of eighty thousand people. I'd finally had the chance to help the team win the game, but we had fallen short. It was a tough loss for the team, especially for Coach Nutt. I truly felt bad for him. I got changed quickly and headed to the bus. Despite the loss, I was pretty darn excited to call my mom and dad and tell them all about the catch.

Three more games on the schedule passed and I didn't log any playing time as a receiver. I was surprised because after my catch at

Arkansas, I thought the coaches were confident in my skills and would give me a little more playing time. I still had my game plan, I still practiced with the starters, and I still had faith in myself and the team.

We traveled to Tennessee to play the Volunteers in front of ninety-seven thousand screaming fans. Unfortunately, we couldn't have started off any slower. In the third quarter, Coach Dickerson pushed me on the back and said, "Go to Z, let's go, and make a play!" I got into the huddle, heard the pass play, and sprinted to the line. It was a five-yard out route and I ran my absolute best out route to date. Jeremiah threw me the ball. I caught it, ran up field, and then dove through a defender for the first down. After getting up, I clapped my hands and then ran back to the huddle. I was angry. I should have been making these catches and plays for this game and the entire season. If I'd been in the game, we might not be losing. After a few running plays, I never saw the field again. I made my second SEC catch in front of a crowd of ninety-seven thousand. I was happy about the catch but disappointed we lost.

For the following game, against LSU, the intensity level was off the charts. There were ninety-two thousand screaming fans this time; I couldn't hear my own voice. The SEC fans were loud, but at LSU, the fans were loud and jumped up and down, shaking the entire stadium. It was an action-packed game and I held field goals and extra points but didn't see any action at receiver. I was the biggest cheerleader on the sideline, praying that I could get in and help the team win the game. I didn't get in as a receiver but continued to stay positive. Playing in front of so many screaming fans was amazing. I think LSU's fans may be some of the most intense in the SEC.

The last game of the season was finally here. It was tradition that we play our biggest rival, Mississippi State, in the Egg Bowl. The winner of the game would receive the Crystal Egg and have bragging rights for the entire year. For me, this game would be the culmination of a lifetime of football. I reminisced about playing in the Wellington Pee Wee football league (WCFL), Wellington ninth grade football, Palm Beach Central, Jacksonville University, and now Ole Miss. I was coming to terms with the thought that this game could be the last I ever played. I wanted to savor every moment as I would a good steak and glass of wine.

At the Tuesday meeting, as we were preparing for our final week of practice, Coach Dickerson made an announcement to all the receivers in the room, "Richie, is going to be the starter this week." I knew Coach Nutt wanted me to play and have a ton of catches in this game. I prepared and practiced as I had done all year. I didn't need to make any changes, because I had always practiced like I was the starter.

The last day of the season was here, and we were at home playing Mississippi State. It was an even more special occasion for coinciding with Senior Day. I was excited because my mom, sister, and brand new nephew came to visit and watch my final game. There was a pregame ceremony, where the families of the senior players were invited on the field, as mine did, congratulating me as a graduate football player.

The announcer called my name and I ran out of the tunnel. It was an emotional moment for me and my family. I hugged my mom, sister, and nephew. My mom whispered in my ear, "No matter what happened these last five years, I couldn't be more proud of you." I said, "Thank you, Mom, I love you. This game's for you."

I wasn't in the starting lineup. As the game progressed, I patiently waited on the sidelines. By halftime, I still had not played receiver. I approached Coach Dickerson and asked if I was going to play. He said "Get ready, you're going in." By the fourth quarter, I was still holding field goals and hadn't played one snap at receiver. My whole family was there; I wanted them to see me catch a pass, but it wasn't meant to be. Before I knew it, the game was over.

I looked in the stands, found my family, and smiled with pride. I ran off the field with my head held high, thinking about my family, my accomplishments, and my future. I was angry that I didn't get to start in my last game as a Rebel, but as I approached the tunnel, my anger disappeared.

Although I never got the chance to be a full-game starter at receiver, I feel like a winner. My experience at Ole Miss was a gift very few athletes even dream of attaining. I earned a D1-scholarship along with a bachelor's degree from the University of Mississippi. I was able to run out of the tunnel in front of more than 102,000 people. I had the opportunity to play in the most prestigious SEC stadiums, and I had catches in front of ninety-seven thousand and eighty-thousand people. I studied hard and was awarded the SEC Scholar-Athlete Award twice. More importantly, I never gave up. I arrived at my destination by learning how to overcome adversity and learning how to win.

Not everything worked out the way I'd planned, but I did learn a great deal about myself and my inner strength. Through my experiences, I developed the confidence that transcends into my personal life and career aspirations. I had a great-paying job in New York City waiting for me before I graduated. If I could earn a D1-scholarship, I could dominate any job.

I hope my experience can be an inspiration to other walk-ons who were told they were "too small" or "not fast enough." If you stay the course, believe in yourself, and put in the hard work, anything is possible. If I can do it, there is hope for you to succeed. I won, and it was all worth it. For more information visit www.EarnaScholarship.com

CPSIA information can be obtained
at www.ICGtesting.com
Printed in the USA
FSOW01n0213290117
30066FS